The New
Military Humanism

The New
Military Humanism

The New Military Humanism

Lessons from Kosovo

Noam Chomsky

New Star Books
Vancouver
1999

New Star Books Ltd.
#107 – 3477 Commercial Street
Vancouver, B.C.
V5N 4E8

This edition for sale in Canada only. Published simultaneously in the United States by Common Courage Press.
Cover design by Erica Bjerning
Printed and bound in the United States of America
1 2 3 4 5 03 02 01 00 99

Canadian Cataloguing in Publication Data

Chomsky, Noam.
       The new military humanism

Includes bibliographical references and index.
ISBN 0-921586-74-4

1.   Kosovo (Serbia) — History — Civil War, 1998- 2. United States — Foreign relations — Balkan Peninsula. 3. Balkan Peninsula — Foreign relations — United States. 4. International relations — Moral and ethical aspects. I. Title.
DR2086.C56 1999   949.7103   C99-910940-5

Contents

CHAPTER 1

"In the Name of Principles and Values"*

The crisis in Kosovo has excited passion and visionary exaltation of a kind rarely witnessed. The events have been portrayed as "a landmark in international relations," opening the gates to a stage of world history with no precedent, a new epoch of moral rectitude under the guiding hand of an "idealistic New World bent on ending inhumanity."[1] This New Humanism, timed fortuitously with a new millennium, will displace the crass and narrow interest politics of a mean-spirited past. Novel conceptions of world order are being forged, interlaced with inspirational lessons about human affairs and global society. These new conceptions are to displace the decaying institutions of world order that have proven to be a "disastrous failure," hence must be discarded in favor of emerging ideas with "innovative but justifiable" departures from earlier norms. The utopianism of earlier generations may be fit only for ridicule, but the visions that are to take their place are genuine, and genuinely inspiring.

---

* Some of the material here has appeared in articles in the U.S. and elsewhere in 1999. For suggestions and assistance, I would like to express particular thanks to Sanjoy Mahajan, David Peterson, and Knut Rognes.

If the picture is true, if it has even a particle of truth, then remarkable prospects lie before us. Material and intellectual resources surely are at hand to overcome terrible tragedies at little cost, with only a modicum of good will. It takes little imagination or knowledge to compile a wish list of tasks to be undertaken that should confer enormous benefits on suffering people. In particular, crimes of the nature and scale of Kosovo are all too easily found, and many could be overcome, at least significantly alleviated, with a fraction of the effort and zeal expended in the cause that has consumed the Western powers and their intellectual cultures in early 1999.

For many good reasons, then, we should seek to locate and identify such tasks and problems and to place them in the forefront of attention and concern. If the high-minded spirit of the liberation of Kosovo has even shreds of authenticity, if at last leaders are acting "in the name of principles and values" that are truly humane as confidently proclaimed (Vaclav Havel), then there will be exciting opportunities to place critically important issues on the agenda of practical and immediate action. And even if reality turns out to fall short of the flattering self-portrait, the effort still has the merit of directing attention to what should be undertaken by those who regard the fine words as something more than cynical opportunism.

Let us try, then, to review and understand what has happened, how and why it is portrayed in the manner we have seen, and what new ventures can be undertaken, with ease, by application of the "universal principles and values espoused by European Union and NATO leaders" and by the commentators who applaud them. Since the range is too vast to sample seriously, let us keep to cases that are similar in essential respects to the tragedy that aroused such intense emotion and commitment in the early months of 1999. Apart from offering a fair test of the New Humanism on its own chosen terrain, such cases are of intrinsic significance and value, at least by elementary moral standards.

To avoid misunderstanding, my aim here is not to contribute to the debate about what should be, or should have been, done in Kosovo, except tangentially. Rather, it is to examine the framework in which events proceeded on their course, with its terrible human toll; and to consider the likely implications of what took place, and of its portrayal and interpretation. That requires an almost wrenching shift from the single-minded concentration of the past months on a corner of the deeply troubled Balkans, which has displaced to the margins other concerns of no little weight. For the reasons just indicated the shift will be limited here to a narrow category of similar tasks and problems, but should properly be extended far beyond.

On March 24, U.S.-led NATO forces launched cruise missiles and bombs at targets throughout the Federal Republic of Yugoslavia (FRY),[2] "plunging America into a military conflict that President Clinton said was necessary to stop ethnic cleansing and bring stability to Eastern Europe," lead stories in the press reported. By bombing the FRY, Clinton informed the nation, "we are upholding our values, protecting our interests, and advancing the cause of peace." "We cannot respond to such tragedies everywhere, but when ethnic conflict turns into ethnic cleansing where we can make a difference, we must try, and that is clearly the case in Kosovo." "Had we faltered" in what the heading of his speech calls "A Just and Necessary War," "the result would have been a moral and strategic disaster. The Albanian Kosovars would have become a people without a homeland, living in difficult conditions in some of the poorest countries in Europe...," a fate that the U.S. cannot tolerate for suffering people. Secretary of State Madeleine Albright had already sounded the alarm, declaring on February 1 "that this kind of thing cannot stand, that you cannot in 1999 have this kind of barbaric ethnic cleansing. It is ultimately better that democracies stand up against this kind of evil."[3]

Clinton's European allies agreed. Under the heading "A New Generation Draws the Line," British Prime Minister Tony Blair declared that this is a new kind of war in which we are fighting "for values," for "a new internationalism where the brutal repression of whole ethnic groups will no longer be tolerated," "for a world where those responsible for such crimes have nowhere to hide." "We are fighting for a world where dictators are no longer able to visit horrific punishments on their own peoples in order to stay in power." We are entering "a new millenium where dictators know that they cannot get away with ethnic cleansing or repress their peoples with impunity." German Foreign Minister Joschka Fischer "became an advocate of what Ulrich Beck, a German intellectual, has called 'NATO's new military humanism'—the notion, defended by Secretary of State Madeleine K. Albright, that the defense of human rights is a form of mission."[4]

"The New Interventionism" was hailed by intellectual opinion and legal scholars who proclaimed a new era in world affairs in which the "enlightened states" will at last be able to use force where they "believe it to be just," discarding "the restrictive old rules" and obeying "modern notions of justice" that they fashion. "The crisis in Kosovo illustrates...America's new willingness to do what it thinks right—international law notwithstanding."[5] Now freed from the shackles of the Cold War and old-fashioned constraints of world order, the enlightened states can dedicate themselves with full vigor to the mission of upholding human rights and bringing justice and freedom to suffering people everywhere, by force if necessary.

The enlightened states are the United States and its British associate, perhaps also others who enlist in their crusades for justice and human rights. Their mission is resisted only by "the defiant, the indolent, and the miscreant," the "disorderly" elements of the world.[6] The rank of enlightenment is apparently conferred by definition. One will search in vain for credible attempts to provide evidence or argument for the critical distinction between enlightened and disorderly, surely not from history. The history is in any event deemed irrelevant by the familiar doctrine of "change of course," which holds that, Yes, in the past we have erred out of naiveté or faulty information, but now we are returning to the traditional path of righteousness. Examination of the record is nothing more than "sound-bites and invectives about Washington's historically evil foreign policy," hence "easy to ignore," we are instructed by one of the most prominent scholar/advocates of the "emerging norms."[7] There is, accordingly, no purpose in asking what might be learned from old, musty stories about the past, even though the decision-making structure and its institutional base remain intact and unchanged.

On June 3, NATO and Serbia reached a Peace Accord. The U.S. triumphantly declared victory, having successfully concluded its "10-week struggle to compel Mr. Milosevic to say uncle." Victory, though not yet peace: the iron fist remains poised until the victors determine that their interpretation of the Peace Accord has been imposed. A broad consensus was articulated by *New York Times* global analyst Thomas Friedman: "From the start the Kosovo problem has been about how we should react when bad things happen in unimportant places." The enlightened states have opened a new millennium by providing an answer to this critical question of the modern era, pursuing the moral principle that "once the refugee evictions began, ignoring Kosovo would be wrong...and therefore using a huge air war for a limited objective was the only thing that made sense."[8]

Inspection of the timing alone shows that this common refrain can hardly be accurate: uncontroversially, the "huge air war" was undertaken before "the refugee evictions began" at a new level, and led to a rapid and vast escalation of evictions and other atrocities, facts reported extensively in Friedman's own journal and others. That much at least is generally recognized. It can be denied only by assuming a determined stance of "intentional ignorance," to borrow the phrase coined by the advocate of the "new internationalism" just quoted, in an incisive report he co-authored on atrocities of U.S. mercenary forces and the State Department reaction to them.[9]

The stance of intentional ignorance has ample precedent. A classic account was given by George Orwell in his preface to *Animal Farm*, which he devoted to the ways in which in free societies "Unpopular ideas can be silenced, and inconvenient facts kept dark, without any need for any official ban." This "sinister" form of "literary censorship" is "largely voluntary," Orwell observed. In part it derives from a good education, which instills the "general tacit agreement that 'it wouldn't do' to mention that particular fact." As a consequence of such intentional ignorance and other factors, "Anyone who challenges the prevailing orthodoxy finds himself silenced with surprising effectiveness." *Animal Farm* is perhaps Orwell's most famous book, the preface one of his least known essays. It remained unpublished, and was discovered only thirty years later, then prominently published, only to return to general oblivion.[10]

While Friedman's own (and conventional) answer to his rhetorical question is untenable, a credible answer appears in the same journal on the same day, though only obliquely. Reporting from Ankara, correspondent Stephen Kinzer writes that "Turkey's best-known human rights advocate [Akin Birdal] entered prison" to serve his sentence for having "urged the state to reach a peaceful settlement with Kurdish rebels."[11] Looking beyond the sporadic and generally uninformative or misleading news reports and commentary, we discover that the sentencing of the courageous president of the Human Rights Association of Turkey is only one episode of a campaign of intimidation and harassment of human rights advocates who are investigating and reporting horrendous atrocities and calling for peaceful resolution of a conflict that has been marked by one of the most savage campaigns of ethnic cleansing and state terror of the 1990s. The campaign has proceeded with mounting fury thanks to the active participation of the leader of the enlightened states, "upholding our values, protecting our interests, and advancing the cause of peace" (in the President's words) in a way that is all too familiar to those who do not prefer intentional ignorance.

We return to details, merely noting here that these events of the 1990s, continuing right now and taking place within NATO and under European jurisdiction, provide a rather striking illustration—far from the only one—of the answer given by the enlightened states to the question of "how we should react when bad things happen in unimportant places": We should react by helping to *escalate the atrocities*, a mission accomplished in Kosovo as well. Such elements of the real world of today raise some rather serious questions about the New Humanism, even if we adopt the doctrine of "change of course" and agree to efface history and its lessons about the institutions of power that reign virtually unchallenged, free to do what they "think right."

By chance, the credible answer to Friedman's question was confirmed, and the contours of the New Humanism clearly delineated, by the second of the two major national journals, the *Washington Post*, in paired editorials at the war's end. One is entitled "Kosovo's

Bumpy Road," the other, "Turkey's Kurdish Opening." The first offers advice to NATO, the second expresses the "hopes" of "friends of Turkey."[12]

In the case of Kosovo, Washington should "show no sympathy" for the villains responsible for savage ethnic cleansing and other atrocities conducted under NATO's bombs. On the contrary, "NATO should intensify its bombing" if it detects any sign of "recalcitrance" in living up to principles that "can't be compromised." Primary among these is the principle that the international peacekeeping force mandated by the U.N. Security Council must have "a NATO general at its command—not an official of the United Nations, the European Union, the Organization for Security and Cooperation in Europe [OSCE] or anybody else."[13] In other words, NATO must firmly reject the Security Council Resolution it had just initiated and signed, which called for an "international security presence" deployed "under U.N. auspices," "with substantial NATO participation" (and no further mention of NATO). And any "recalcitrance" in submitting to NATO's unilateral decisions should be met with renewed violence by the stern disciplinarian.

In the case of Turkey, the story is different. Washington should most definitely "show sympathy" for the villains responsible for savage ethnic cleansing and other atrocities against the Kurds, surely comparable to Serbian crimes in Kosovo and not carried out under NATO's bombs. Not a very surprising conclusion, since Washington occupies a prominent place among the villains. In the case of Turkey and the Kurds, it is the "captive leader of the Kurdish separatist movement," Abdullah Ocalan, who is "widely held responsible for the death of thousands [more accurately, tens of thousands] in the Kurds' war with the Turks." The term "widely held" excludes the leading international human rights organizations and independent scholarship but includes Ankara and Washington. Similarly, and with comparable merit, in Belgrade and perhaps Moscow it is the guerrilla forces of the Albanian separatist movement that are "widely held responsible" for death of thousands in the Albanians' war with the Serbs in the period before the NATO bombing, of course the relevant period for an assessment of the decision to bomb. There were indeed atrocities during this peri-od; we return to Washington's account of them. No serious analyst regards them as remotely comparable to the atrocities carried out by "the NATO-oriented Turkish armed forces"—the editors' term for the Turkish military forces armed and trained by Washington, with an increasing flow of arms as atrocities mounted and the Clinton Administration was bent on demonstrating "America's new willing-ness to do what it thinks right."

The editors issue no call for bombing Ankara or Washington. Rather, "friends of Turkey must hope it can muster the courage to broaden its perspective and to conduct an honest exploration of the Ocalan initiative" for a peaceful settlement, referring to the peace initiative of the "captive leader" that has been rejected for seven years by the Turkish government and its friends in Washington, and still is, as "Turkey's best-known human rights advocate" had learned just days before. If Turkey chooses "to treat its national can-cer, the problem of the aggrieved Kurdish minority," the editors continue, then it will no longer be "at odds with the humane democratic values of the Western nations whose company it val-ues," notably the humane values of the nation that provides Turkey with a huge flow of lethal weapons "to treat its national cancer" in the manner Washington prefers. "For the Turks, accommodating the Kurds won't be easy," the editors recognize. Kurds now ask for the "cultural and linguistic rights" that have been denied them (unlike Kosovo), but later "some of them" may go on to ask "for autonomy and self-determination" (like the Kosovo Albanians for many years). Hence Turkey's leaders merit sympathetic understand-ing from their friends in Washington.

A fuller account, to which we briefly return, draws the contrast even more sharply between state terror conducted with the approval and avid support of the enlightened states, most promi-nently their leader, and state terror that is villainous and must be severely punished because it conflicts with their demands. There are no novelties here. Merely to give a single example, a few years earlier the editors of the same journal were advising their govern-ment on more effective means to "fit Nicaragua back into a Central American mode" and impose "reasonable conduct by a regional standard"—that is, to fit Nicaragua into the mode of the murderous terror states backed by Washington, and to adopt their "regional standard" of vicious atrocities that vastly exceeded any crimes attributed to the Nicaraguan enemy, apart from the crime of disobedience to the ruler of the hemisphere.[14]

The stance is in fact conventional, not only among the leaders of the enlightened states but also among their enemies and predecessors. *Pravda* in the old days made similar distinctions, again with comparable merit. The historical record should be familiar.

These are among the most important questions raised by the Balkans war of 1999. They remain out of sight—within the "enlightened states," at least. Elsewhere, they are readily perceived, over a broad spectrum. To select several remote points for illustration, a prominent Israeli commentator on military and strategic affairs sees the enlightened states as "a danger to the world." He describes their "new rules of the game" as a reversion to the colonial era, with the resort to force "cloaked in moralistic righteousness" as the rich and powerful do "what seems to them to be justified." Another commentator, head of the Center Party and wife of the ex-Chief of Staff, writes that "power won and peace lost": "the rules of the game are far from having been changes...In this story there are no good and evil, only very evil and less evil." At a very different point on the spectrum, Alexander Solzhenitsyn, a Western idol when he is saying the right things, offers a succinct definition of the New Humanism: "The aggressors have kicked aside the U.N., opening a new era where might is right." To take a last example, Vuk Draskovic, deposed by Milosevic for opposing his war policy and calling for peace protests, received high praise in the West as the Good Serb, the voice of reason and independence in the government and the hope for Serbian democracy in a post-Milosevic era. His opposition was based on Solzhenitsyn's thesis: "we must recognize the fact that the world today is often ruled by the rule of power, and not the rule of law. We must be very brave and approach compromise."[15]

We return to a broader sample, representing a good part of the world's population, perhaps a majority, one respected hawkish policy analyst alleges. They might agree with an observation by the prominent and influential—though little celebrated—radical pacifist A.J. Muste:

The problem after a war is with the victor. He thinks he has just proved that war and violence pay. Who will now teach him a lesson?[16]

"There should be no indulging in illusions about [NATO] aiming at defending Kosovars," Solzhenitsyn added: "if the protection of the oppressed was their real concern, they could have been defending for example the miserable Kurds, who have been torn by different countries for about 40 or 50 years, and are subject to extermination"—an exaggeration, but hardly worse than the extreme forms of Holocaust revisionism that compare the horrendous Serb atrocities that followed the bombing to Hitler's genocidal policies, a comparison that would cut a wide swath were it taken seriously. NATO tolerates Turkey's ethnic cleansing and terror because it is their "paying ally," Solzhenitsyn adds, confirming the judgment in the West about the "goodwill Turkey has built up over its actions in the Kosovo crisis" as it pays its dues once again, this time joining in the "moralistic righteousness" of the rich and powerful over Turkish-style atrocities.[17]

The conjunction elicits no notice, a fact that might interest people genuinely concerned about the moral and intellectual culture of the enlightened states.

The larger issues highlighted by the most recent of the wars of Yugoslav secession came into focus with the fading of the Cold War. Central among these is the claimed right of intervention on the part of states or alliances on humanitarian grounds, which extends the scope of legitimated use of force. There is general agreement on the timing, but the conclusions about "humanitarian intervention" are phrased in different ways, reflecting the evaluation of the intent and likely consequences of the "emerging norms of justified intervention."[18]

The enlarged options are of two kinds: those carried out under United Nations auspices and in conformity with the U.N. Charter, which is agreed to be the foundation of international law in the post-World War II period; and those carried out unilaterally, with no Security Council authorization, by states or alliances (the U.S. or NATO for example, or the Warsaw Pact in earlier years). If sufficiently powerful, arrogant, and internally well-disciplined, such alliances may designate themselves "the international community" (standard practice in the U.S. and often NATO generally). Questions arise about the first category, but that is not our topic here. Rather, we are concerned with the "emerging norms of justified intervention" by states or alliances that do not seek or are not granted authorization from the international community, but that use force because "they believe it to be just." In practice, that reduces to "America's new willingness to do what it thinks right," apart from operations in "unimportant countries" of no concern to the reigning global superpower (for example, peacekeeping interventions of the West African states, which received retroactive authorization from the United Nations).

From one perspective, the extended scope of intervention has always been legitimate, indeed meritorious, but was obstructed during the Cold War because "the defiant, the indolent, and the miscreant" who resist the mission were then able to rely for support on the Communist powers, dedicated to subversion and insurrection as they sought to conquer the world.[19] With the Cold War over, the "disorderly" can no longer impede the good works of the enlightened states, and the New Humanism can therefore flourish under their wise and just leadership.

From a contrasting perspective, "the new interventionism" is replaying an old record. It is an updated variant of traditional practices that were impeded in a bipolar world system that allowed some space for nonalignment—a concept that effectively vanishes when one of the two poles disappears.[20] The Soviet Union, and to some extent China, set limits on the actions of the Western powers in their traditional domains, not only by virtue of the military deterrent, but also because of their occasional willingness, however opportunistic, to lend support to targets of Western subversion and aggression (in practice, overwhelmingly U.S.-based, for obvious reasons of power). With the Soviet deterrent in decline, the Cold War victors are more free to exercise their will under the cloak of good intentions but in pursuit of interests that have a very familiar ring outside the realm of enlightenment.

The self-described bearers of enlightenment happen to be the rich and powerful, the inheritors of the colonial and neocolonial systems of global dominion: they are the North, the First World. The disorderly miscreants who defy them have been at the other end of the stick: they are the South, the Third World—the "developing" or "less developed countries" or "transitional economies," all notions with a heavy ideological overlay. The division is not sharp and clear; nothing is in the domain of human affairs. But the tendencies are hard to miss, and they suggest some reasons for the difference of perspective in interpretation of "the emerging norms of justified intervention."

The conflict of interpretation is difficult to resolve if history is declared irrelevant and the present scene is glimpsed only through the filters established by the enlightened states, which transmit the evil deeds of official enemies while blocking unwanted images: to take the most obvious current illustration, atrocities pass through unhindered, even magnified, if they are attributable to Belgrade, but not if they trace back to Ankara/Washington. As long as these restrictions on inquiry are observed, the preferred interpretation has at least a chance to survive inspection.

The general questions will be deferred to the end (chapters 6 and 7), but they lie in the not very distant background of the consideration of particular humanitarian crises: Kosovo Albanians, Kurds of Turkey, and others. If we hope to understand anything about the world, in such particular cases we should ask why decisions on forceful intervention are made one way or another by the states with the power to exercise their judgment and will. The questions were raised at the outset of the recent revival of the thesis that the enlightened states should use force when they "believe it to be just"—"revival" is the right term, because of its well-known and distinguished origins. In the 1993 American Academy Conference on Emerging Norms, one of the most distinguished figures in the academic discipline of international relations, Ernest Haas, raised a simple and cogent question, which has since received a clear and instructive answer. He observed that NATO was then intervening in Iraq and Bosnia to protect Kurds and Muslims, and asked: "will NATO take the same interventionist view if and when Turkey begins to lean more heavily on its Kurdish insurgents?" The question poses a clear test of the New Humanism: Is it guided by power interests, or by humanitarian concern? Is the resort to force undertaken "in the name of principles and values," as professed? Or are we witnessing something more crass and familiar?

The test was a good one, and the answer was not long in coming. As Haas raised the question, Turkey was leaning much more heavily on the Kurdish population of the Southeast while rejecting offers of peaceful settlement that would permit cultural and linguistic rights. Very shortly the operation escalated to extremes of ethnic cleansing and state terror. NATO took a very definite "interventionist view," in particular NATO's leader, which intervened decisively to escalate the atrocities. The ideological institutions adapted in the manner just illustrated, also following a familiar path.

The implications concerning the larger issues seem rather clear, particularly when we compare this "interventionist view" to the one adopted for the Kosovo crisis, a lesser one on moral grounds, not only for reasons of scale (crucially and dramatically, prior to the decision to bombard the FRY) but also because it is outside the bounds and jurisdiction of the NATO powers and their institutions, unlike Turkey, which is squarely within. The two cases differ sharply on a different dimension, however: Serbia is one of those disorderly miscreants that impede the institution of the U.S.-dominated global system, while Turkey is a loyal client state that contributes substantially to this project. Again, the factors that drive policy do not seem hard to discern, and the "North-South" divisions over the larger issues and their interpretation seem to fall into place as well.

The leading issues that arise are not resolved by a single example, and this one case itself requires careful elaboration and inquiry. The natural conclusions have a prima facie plausibility, however. When we look more closely we find, I think, that these conclusions come through loud and clear. We also find that they are reinforced by a broad range of considerations that reach well beyond military intervention, including international financial arrangements, trade agreements, control over technology and material and human resources, and the whole array of devices by which power is concentrated and organized, and applied to institute systems of domination and control.

These are the kinds of questions that should be in the immediate background as we turn to the "unimportant places" of elite perception, ask what is happening there and why, and most importantly, why power systems make the choices they do and what we should be doing about those choices.

The New Humanism was given forceful expression in the Clinton Doctrine, outlined by National Security Advisor Anthony Lake, the Administration's leading intellectual: "Throughout the Cold War we contained a global threat to market democracies," but now we can move on to "consolidate the victory of democracy and open markets." Press commentators had already recognized that "with the end of the cold war...interventionism has won out"; the issue that remains is whether policy will be guided by Bush-style balance of power realism or the Clinton-Lake "'new-Wilsonian' view in which the United States uses its monopoly on power to intervene in other countries to promote democracy."[21]

Several years of Clinton's "new-Wilsonianism" convinced observers that American foreign policy had entered a "noble phase" with a "saintly glow," though more sober voices warned that by "granting idealism a near exclusive hold on our foreign policy" we might neglect our own interests in the service of others. It is between these poles that serious discussion largely proceeds.[22]

Though the new era opened with the fall of the Berlin Wall in November 1989 according to the logic of the doctrine, it is only a decade later, with the NATO intervention to protect Kosovo Albanians from brutal ethnic cleansing, that its contours have been firmly established. The NATO bombings are therefore a defining moment in world affairs, the first time in history when the "saintly glow" of policy shines through for all to see—"evidently" and "obviously," respected voices announce.[23] It is symbolically appropriate that this remarkable new era should break forth at the opening of the third millennium of the Christian era, perhaps to be the theme of inspiring rhetoric as the day approaches.

Even skeptics agreed, long before Kosovo, that "clearly, something important is going on."[24] That much is surely true, and the flood of impassioned rhetoric accompanying the NATO intervention of 1999 underscores its importance.

Any attempt to address the topic should distinguish clearly between two questions: (1) what should be done, and (2) what is being done and why. The answers to question (2) bear on the choice of action, but do not determine it. It is easy to find historical examples in which actions undertaken on cynical grounds, or worse, had beneficial consequences that were plausibly anticipated, so it might have been appropriate to support such actions whatever the motives and goals. It is more difficult to find examples of state actions undertaken on humanitarian grounds, but insofar as such exist, they might have (anticipated) beneficial or harmful consequences. Though the merest truisms, these distinctions should be kept in mind in the present case as in all others.

Question (2) is of particular importance when it is elevated to extraordinary heights, as in the contemporary rhetoric of political leaders and commentators with regard to the New Humanism and its exemplification in NATO's Balkan intervention. It is that question that will concern me here. We can expect with some confidence that cases of the kind discussed will continue to arise. Valuable lessons can be learned by examining question (2) against the background of the broader range of questions raised by the New Humanism of the new millennium.

Even a cursory examination shows that the proclamations of the New Humanism are at best highly dubious. The narrowest focus, on the NATO intervention in Kosovo alone, suffices to undermine the lofty pronouncements. A broader look at the contemporary world powerfully reinforces the conclusion, and brings forth with stark clarity "the values" that are actually being upheld. If we deviate further from the marching orders that issue from Washington and London and allow the past to enter the discussion, we quickly discover that the "New Generation" is the old generation, and that the "new internationalism" replays old and unpleasant records. The actions of distinguished forebears, as well as the justifications offered and their merits, should also give us pause. High level planning for the new millennium, at least some of which is available to those who choose to know, adds further warnings for people who really are committed to the values that are proclaimed.

The British press reported that Britain's phase of the NATO bombing was to be called "Operation Agricola."[25] If so, the choice is apt, and a tribute to Britain's classical education. Apart from being a major criminal who helped cure the country's Celtic infection, Agricola was the father-in-law of Tacitus, noted for his observation that "crime once exposed had no refuge but in audacity," and for his famous description of the Roman empire: "Brigands of the world, they create a desolation and call it peace."

Let us begin by keeping to the rules and focusing attention on the designated case: Serb atrocities in Kosovo, which are quite real, and often ghastly. We immediately discover that the bombing was not undertaken in "response" to ethnic cleansing and to "reverse" it, as leaders alleged.[26] With full awareness of the likely consequences, Clinton and Blair decided in favor of a war that led to a radical escalation of ethnic cleansing along with other deleterious effects.

In the year before the bombing, according to NATO sources, about 2000 people had been killed in Kosovo and several hundred thousand had become internal refugees. The humanitarian catastrophe was overwhelmingly attributable to Yugoslav police and military forces, the main victims being ethnic Albanians, commonly assumed to constitute about 90% of the population by the 1990s.

Prior to the bombing, and for two days following its onset, the United Nations High Commissioner for Refugees (UNHCR) reported no data on refugees, though many Kosovars—Albanian and Serb—had been leaving the province for years, and entering as well, sometimes as a direct consequence of the Balkan wars, sometimes for economic and other reasons.[27] After three days of bombing, UNHCR reported on March 27 that 4000 had fled Kosovo to Albania and Macedonia, the two neighboring countries. Until April 1 the UNHCR provided no daily figures on refugees, according to the *New York Times*. By April 5, the *Times* reported that "more than 350,000 have left Kosovo since March 24," relying on UNHCR figures, while unknown numbers of Serbs fled north to Serbia to escape the increased violence from the air and on the ground. After the war, it was reported that half the Serb population had "moved out when the NATO bombing began." There have been varying estimates of the number of refugees within Kosovo before the NATO bombing. Cambridge University Law Professor Marc Weller, Legal Advisor to the Kosova (Kosovo Albanian) Delegation at the 1999 Rambouillet Conference on Kosovo, reports that after the withdrawal of the international monitors (KVM, Kosovo Verification Mission) on March 19, 1999, "within a few days the number of displaced had again risen to over 200,000." Basing himself on U.S. intelligence, House Intelligence Committee Chair Porter Goss gave the estimate of 250,000 internally displaced. The UNHCR reported on March 11 that "more than 230,000 people remain displaced within Kosovo."[28]

By the time of the peace accord of June 3, the UNHCR reported 671,500 refugees beyond the borders of the FRY, in addition to 70,000 in Montenegro and 75,000 who went to other countries.[29] To these we may add the unknown numbers displaced within Kosovo, perhaps some 2–300,000 in the year before the bombing, far more afterwards, with varying estimates; and according to the Yugoslav Red Cross, over a million displaced within Serbia after the bombing,[30] along with many who left Serbia.

The numbers reported from Kosovo are, unfortunately, all too familiar. To mention only two cases that are prime illustrations of "our values" in the 1990s, the refugee toll prior to the NATO bombing is similar to the State Department estimate for Colombia in the same year (we return to this instructive comparison); and the UNHCR totals at the war's end are about the same as the number of Palestinians who fled or were expelled in 1948, another policy issue that is very much alive today. In that case, refugees numbered about 750,000, 85% of the population, with over 400 villages levelled, and ample violence. The comparison was not overlooked in the Israeli press, which described Kosovo as Palestine 1948 with TV cameras (Gideon Levi). Foreign Minister Ariel Sharon warned that if "NATO's aggression" is "legitimized," the next step might be a call for autonomy and links to the Palestinian Authority for Galilee—the "underpopulated Galilee" (Irving Howe), meaning that it has too few Jews and too many Arabs. Others comment that "the Serbs could almost have studied Israeli tactics in 1948 in their village destruction campaign, except of course the Palestinians had no NATO to back them up" (Ian Williams, a fervent supporter of the NATO bombing).[31]

To be sure, the Palestinians could appeal to a U.N. Resolution that guaranteed them the right of return or, if they refused, compensation: U.N. 194 of Dec. 11, 1948, which spelled out the intended meaning of Article 13(2) of the Universal Declaration of Human Rights (UD), adopted the preceding day. But such guarantees depend on the will of the superpowers, primarily the United States, which regarded the U.N. Resolution as a mere formality. Meanwhile Article 13(2) became perhaps the best-known Article of the UD as it was converted into an ideological weapon against the Soviet enemy for violating it by refusing to allow Jews to leave, a weapon wielded with great indignation, passion, and "moralistic righteousness," and always with omission of the final words guaranteeing the right to return to one's own country, a display of audacity that might have impressed Tacitus, and that proceeded annually without a false note or raised eyebrow, an interesting illustration of Orwell's maxim. Nonetheless, support for Article 13(2) remained official policy until it was rescinded by President Clinton, who formalized his stand that unworthy victims should "become a people without a homeland, living in difficult conditions in some of the poorest countries" in the world, far poorer than those of Europe.[32]

Clinton's formal renunciation of Article 13 of the UD received the usual notice—zero—which is fitting: U.S. isolation in the United Nations is so routine as perhaps not to merit report. And when the world is out of step, as it so commonly is, its position can be disregarded. Thus today, reporting on violence in Lebanon that is traced to the miserable conditions of Palestinians living there in hopeless exile, the *New York Times* can report that "The authorities [in Lebanon] have always insisted that…the Palestinians must be allowed to return to the lands they fled in 1948." So the authorities in Lebanon have, though it would be more informative to point out that Israel and the U.S. (since Clinton) are alone in rejecting Resolution 194 and the Article of the UD that it spells out. Adopting the same mode of shaping history, the report goes on to describe how "cross-border attacks on Israel by Palestinian militias prompted the Israeli invasion of 1982," a conventional U.S. rendition of the fact that cross-border attacks had long ceased apart from the murderous attacks in the other direction, as Israel desperately sought to elicit some terrorist actions that could serve as a pretext for its planned U.S.-backed invasion. One can hardly accuse the reporter of deceit, however: that has long been the official line in the U.S.—though not in Israel, where the truth has been openly and publicly recognized from the first days of its invasion of Lebanon in 1982.[33]

Such examples, which are legion, should not be stored in dusty cabinets but rather placed on the front shelf, in plain view, as we watch the next chapters of history unfold.

The distinction between worthy and unworthy victims is traditional, as is its basis, remote from any moral principle apart from the rights demanded by power and privilege. Documentation on the matter is rich and compelling, but excluded from polite company by Orwell's maxim.[34]

As noted, Clinton's opposition to the right of return for victims of large scale ethnic cleansing left Washington in its familiar position of isolation in the international community, and in the equally familiar position of simultaneously rejecting the principles of the UD (for unworthy victims, Palestinians and many others) and passionately upholding them (for worthy victims, now Kosovo Albanians). Though readily understood in terms of power interests, the distinctions, when noticed at all, are portrayed as "double standards" or "mistakes" in respectable commentary. Attention to the facts reveals that there is a single standard, the one that great powers typically observe, and that although plans may go awry (aggressors have been defeated, etc.), the "mistakes" are overwhelmingly tactical.

The worthy/unworthy categories are often identified in complex and shifting ways. Thus Saddam Hussein was a friend and ally and proper recipient of substantial military and other aid from the U.S./U.K. (and other enlightened states) while he was only gassing Kurds, torturing dissidents, and otherwise committing the worst crimes of his career. But he instantly became a reincarnation of

Attila the Hun when he disobeyed orders in August 1990, then regaining his favored status after the Gulf war, in March 1991, when he was tacitly authorized by the U.S. to conduct the murderous suppression of a Shi'ite uprising in the South and a Kurdish uprising in the North (Washington's support was justified in order to preserve "stability," commentators thoughtfully intoned). He reverted to devil as policy shifted to destruction of Iraqi society while strengthening its dictator. Such policy shifts, which are common, require considerable agility on the part of those committed to Orwell's maxim.[35]

Continuing with Kosovo, refugees reported that immediately after the bombing began, the terror reached the capital city of Pristina, mostly spared before, and provided credible accounts of large-scale destruction of villages, brutal atrocities, and a radical increase in generation of refugees, perhaps an effort to expel the Albanian population. Similar reports, generally quite credible, were prominently featured throughout the media and journals, in extensive and often horrifying detail, the usual practice in the case of worthy victims under attack by official enemies.

One index of the effects of "the huge air war" was offered by Robert Hayden, director of the Center for Russian and East European Studies of the University of Pittsburgh: "the casualties among Serb civilians in the first three weeks of the war are higher than all of the casualties on both sides in Kosovo in the three months that led up to this war, and yet those three months were supposed to be a humanitarian catastrophe."[36] Admittedly, casualties among Serb civilians amount to little in the context of the jingoist hysteria that was whipped up for a war against Serbs. But the toll among Albanians in the first three weeks, estimated at the time in the hundreds though presumably much higher, was surely far beyond that of the preceding three months and probably the preceding years.

On March 27, U.S.-NATO Commanding General Wesley Clark announced that it was "entirely predictable" that Serb terror and violence would intensify after the NATO bombing. On the same day, State Department spokesperson James Rubin said that "The United States is extremely alarmed by reports of an escalating pattern of Serbian attacks on Kosovar Albanian civilians," now attrib-uted in large part to paramilitary forces. Shortly after, Clark report-ed again that he was not surprised by the sharp escalation of Serb terror after the bombing: "The military authorities fully anticipated the vicious approach that Milosevic would adopt, as well as the ter-rible efficiency with which he would carry it out."[37]

General Clark's phrase "entirely predictable" is an overstate-ment. Nothing in human affairs is "entirely predictable," surely not the effects of extreme violence. But what happened at once was highly likely. As observed by Carnes Lord of the Fletcher School of Law and Diplomacy, formerly a Bush Administration national secu-rity advisor, "enemies often react when shot at," and "though Western officials continue to deny it, there can be little doubt that the bombing campaign has provided both motive and opportunity for a wider and more savage Serbian operation than what was first envisioned"[38]—by some, at least, if not the Commanding General.

The outcome was not unanticipated in Washington. On March 5, Italian Prime Minister Massimo D'Alema visited Washington, warning Clinton that if Milosevic did not capitulate immediately, "the result...would be 300,000 to 400,000 refugees passing into Albania"—and, he feared, Italy. Clinton turned to National Security Advisor Sandy Berger, who told D'Alema that in that case "NATO will keep bombing," with still more horrific results. House Intelligence Committee Chair Porter Goss informed the media that "Our intelligence community warned us months and days before [the bombing] that we would have a virtual explosion of refugees over the 250,000 that was expected as of last year [pre-bombing], that the Serb resolve would increase, that the conflict would spread, and that there would be ethnic cleansing." As far back as 1992, European monitors in Macedonia had "predicted a sudden, massive influx of ethnic Albanian refugees if hostilities spread into Kosovo."[39]

The reasons for these expectations are clear enough: people "react when shot at"—not by garlanding the attackers with flowers, and not where the attacker is strong, but where they are strong: in this case, on the ground, not by sending jet planes to bomb Washington and London. It takes no particular genius to reach these conclusions, nor access to secret intelligence. The overt NATO threat of direct invasion made the brutal reaction even more likely, again for reasons that could hardly have escaped Clinton, Blair, their associates, and commentators. One may recall how the U.S. reacted during World War II when it was never under the remotest threat of Japanese attack—and in fact, had not been under any threat since the war of 1812.

The threat of bombing presumably had already led to an increase in atrocities, though evidence is slight. The withdrawal of U.S.-led KVM on March 19 in preparation for the bombing presumably had the same consequence, again predictably. "The monitors were widely seen as the only remaining brake on Yugoslav troops," the *Washington Post* observed in a retrospective account; and releasing the brake, it must have been assumed, would lead to disaster. Other accounts agree. A subsequent detailed retrospective in the *New York Times* concludes that "The Serbs began attacking Kosovo Liberation Army strongholds on March 19, but their attack kicked into high gear on March 24, the night NATO began bombing Yugoslavia."[40] It would take a heavy dose of "intentional ignorance" to interpret the facts as mere coincidence.

Serbia officially opposed the withdrawal of the monitors. In a March 23 Resolution responding to the NATO Rambouillet ultimatum, the Serb National Assembly declared: "We also condemn the withdrawal of the OSCE Kosovo Verification Mission. There is not a single reason for this but to put the withdrawal into the service of blackmail and threats to our country."[41] The National Assembly Resolution was not reported by the mainstream media, which also did not publish the terms of the Rambouillet Agreement, though the latter was identified throughout the war as right and just. It was "the peace process," emphasis on *the*, a term used reflexively to refer to Washington's stand whatever it may be (often efforts to undermine diplomacy), a practice that has been particularly instructive with regard to the Middle East and Central America.[42]

We return to the crucial documents that laid out the diplomatic options as the U.S./U.K. decided to bomb in accord with the dictates of the "new internationalism"—the Rambouillet Agreement and the Serb National Assembly Resolution—merely noting here that both were kept under wraps, unavailable to the general population, though some of the crucial facts were released after the Peace Accord rendered them irrelevant to the threat of democracy, and it was even discovered that they were "fatally flawed" and had undermined a course of diplomacy that "might have won the day" without the terrible human consequences of "brute force," all matters to which we return.

The bombing was undertaken five days after the withdrawal of the monitors with the rational expectation that "the result" would be atrocities and ethnic cleansing, and a "sudden, massive" flight and expulsion of Albanians. That indeed happened, even if the scale may have come as a surprise to some, though the Commanding General apparently expected nothing less.

CHAPTER 2

Before the Bombing

Under Marshall Tito's rule, Kosovars had a considerable measure of self-rule, particularly from the 1960s and under the 1974 constitution, which gave Kosovo an ambiguous status, "somewhat between an autonomous province and a federation member-state," a dissident Serb scholar comments.[1] The distinction is important: member-states of the Federation had at least a technical right to secede.

In 1981, an Albanian Professor at the University of Pristina concluded from broad travel and study that "not a single national minority in the world has achieved the rights that the Albanian nationality enjoys in Socialist Yugoslavia."[2] The situation had, however, begun to deteriorate after Tito's death a year earlier, in May 1980. In 1989 Kosovo's autonomy was effectively rescinded in a series of constitutional revisions and administrative steps by the Serbian government under the leadership of Slobodan Milosevic. These reinstituted the basic terms of the 1963 federal constitution, restoring Serbia's direct control; the same moves affected Vojvodina, the home of the Hungarian minority.

The reversion to the post-World War II arrangements was strongly opposed by Kosovo Albanians, and seems to have had comparably strong support among Serbs. The most prominent Yugoslav dissident, Milovan Djilas, who had long been justly admired in the West for his courageous stand against Tito's dictatorship, expressed his agreement with Milosevic's "policy of sorting out the relations of Serbia with her Provinces" and granting "the largest nation" in Yugoslavia (the Serbs) "the status which all national minorities enjoy." "Wipe away Kosovo from the Serb mind and soul and we are no more," he said. Meanwhile the official press agency of Albania declared that "There is no Albania without Kosovo and vice versa," so that we must "demolish the border dividing Albanians from Albanians," a sentiment overwhelmingly shared by Kosovo Albanians. "The political goal" of the post-1989 restoration, Vickers writes, "was to prevent Kosovo's secession and help the physical return of Serbs to the province," many of whom had left under what they described as "the genocidal tactics of the Albanian separatists." "The term 'Kosovo' has been used as a metaphor by both Serbs and Albanians for the 'suffering and injustices' inflicted upon their nations throughout their turbulent history," in which one side or the other has held the whip.[3]

The outcome of the Serbian programs has been described as "Kosovar Apartheid" (Vickers), "a Serbian version of Apartheid" in Kosovo (James Hooper).[4] But the Kosovo Albanians "confounded the international community," Hooper continues, "by eschewing a war of national liberation, embracing instead the nonviolent approach espoused by leading Kosovo intellectual Ibrahim Rugova and constructing a parallel civil society." For this achievement they were rewarded by "polite audiences and rhetorical encouragement from Western governments," but nothing more. In one important case, at a London conference on the Balkans crises hosted by the British government and the U.N., "the entire new Kosovar political élite turned up, only to be relegated to a side room where they had to be content with watching the proceedings on a TV monitor," "an enormous humiliation."[5]

The nonviolent strategy "lost its credibility" after the Dayton accords on Bosnia in November 1995, Hooper writes, expressing the standard conclusion of specialists. At Dayton the U.S. effectively partitioned Bosnia-Herzegovina between an eventual greater Croatia and greater Serbia, after having roughly equalized the balance of terror by providing arms and training for the forces of Franjo Tudjman, the Croatian counterpart to Milosevic, and having supported his violent expulsion of hundreds of thousands of Serbs from Krajina, acknowledged to be the most extreme single case of ethnic cleansing in the horrendous wars of secession in Yugoslavia but one that has not yet called for indictments[6]; if it ever does, these will be narrowly focused, given the roots of the policy. Thousands of expelled Serbs were sent to Kosovo.

With the sides more or less balanced, and exhausted, the U.S. took over, displacing the Europeans who had been assigned the dirty work—to their considerable annoyance. "In deference to Milosevic," Hooper writes, the U.S. "excluded Kosovo Albanian delegates" from the Dayton negotiations and "avoided discussion of the Kosovo problem." "The reward for nonviolence was international neglect"; more significantly, U.S. neglect. The result, Hooper concludes, was "the rise of the guerrilla Kosovo Liberation Army (KLA/UCK) and expansion of popular support for an armed independence struggle." In May 1999, by the time the KLA had become virtually the ground forces of the NATO military operations, it appointed as its military commander Agim Ceku, an architect of the Krajina ethnic cleansing operation. British correspondent Robert Fisk asked NATO's official spokesperson, Britain's Jamie Shea, for NATO's reaction. "Mr Shea said he had no comment," Fisk reported, "because 'NATO has no direct contact with the KLA'."[7]

With or without direct contact, NATO was openly supporting KLA cross-border attacks, using the guerrillas to draw Serb forces into the open so that they could be killed by U.S. bombing. In one case that elicited considerable self-congratulation, some 4–500 or more Yugoslav soldiers were reported to have been killed "by a US B-52 bomber that caught them massing in a field" to repel a cross-border attack. "The B-52 was ordered to drop a large number of cluster bombs," weapons that are arguably banned by international conventions that the U.S. has refused to sign and that continue to exact a huge civilian toll for many years after.[8]

In September 1990, an illegal parliamentary session had declared Kosovo an independent state, adopting the "Kacanik Constitution," which at that time still "sought the solution to Kosovo's status within the framework of Yugoslavia" (Vickers). A year later, the situation had changed with the secession of Slovenia and Croatia and their quick recognition by the West—in the latter case, without concern for the rights of the Serbian minority, a recipe for disaster, as widely noted. In the wake of these events, in September 1991 the Kosovar Parliament approved a "Resolution on Independence and Sovereignty of Kosovo." A few days later, the decision was approved by close to 100% of the 87% of eligible voters who took part in a clandestine referendum, illegal according to the Serb authorities but not disrupted. On October 19, the Parliament declared the independence of Kosovo. A week before, political parties of Kosovo Albanians had signed a declaration calling for "unification of all Albanians." Albania responded by officially recognizing the "Republic of Kosovo" as a sovereign and independent state in late October. In a presidential and parliamentary election of May 1992, Rugova, the sole candidate, was elected President with 99.5% of the vote, and his Democratic League of Kosovo (LDK) won 75% of the seats in Parliament.[9]

Journalist/historian Tim Judah describes Rugova's LDK as "a curious mirror image to Milosevic's SPS [Socialist Party of Serbia], for so long the dominating power in Serbian politics." The LDK "brooks little dissent and those that challenge it are howled down in LDK publications and can even be ostracised in the tight-knit Albanian community"; and "woe betide any Albanian family or shop or businessman who will not pay his dues to Kosova's tax collectors."[10] Meanwhile, for "Albanians in Kosovo…Serbian rule is an occupation." Large numbers of Albanians and Serbs had left because of repression and economic hardship.[11] According to *New York Times* correspondent Chris Hedges, who covered the region, "between 1966 and 1989 an estimated 130,000 Serbs left the province because of frequent harassment and discrimination by the Kosovar Albanian majority."[12]

"Serbs argue that Kosovo is kept under such a tight regime because the LDK is a separatist party," Judah reports, a fact that the LDK "proclaims…loud and clear," having declared "national independence" with the support of the vast majority of Albanians. Rugova's policy was "waiting until there are no more Serbs left in Kosovo or their numbers become so insignificant that somehow the province falls to his people like a ripe fruit." The issue is not "merely a question of human rights," as "many westerners in search of simplicity like to portray the Kosovo problem." Favoring a Serbian victory in the conflict, the Kosovar Albanian leadership "in no way stuck up for the Croats and Bosnian Muslims," much as "in their hearts they wanted to see the Serbs defeated and humiliated." The reason, Judah argues, is that "they did not want the international community to uphold the principle that Yugoslavia's old republican borders could turn into new inviolable international ones," leaving Kosovo a province "trapped inside Serbia" rather than a Republic, with the theoretical right of secession under the Titoist framework. In the Yugoslav elections of 1992, Kosovo Albanians abstained; the LDK denounced participants as "traitors." Vickers concludes that

> the million Albanian votes would undoubtedly have ousted Milosevic, but as the Kosovar leadership admitted at the time, they did not want him to go. Unless Serbia continued to be labelled as profoundly evil—and they themselves, by virtue of being anti-Serb, as the good guys—they were unlikely to achieve their goals. It would have been a disaster for them if a peacemonger like [opposition candidate Milan] Panic had restored human rights, since this would have left them with nothing but a bare political agenda to change borders.

In 1992–93, the Serbian president of Yugoslavia, Dobrica Cosic, proposed in "discreet contacts with Kosovo Albanian leaders" that the territory be partitioned, separating itself from Serbia apart from "a number of Serbian enclaves." But the proposal "was rejected by Albanian leaders" of Rugova's Republic of Kosovo.[13] As noted, the Republic had already declared independence, also setting up a parallel educational and health system that continued to function under Serbian repression while Rugova travelled abroad to lobby for independence, joining the government-in-exile, without losing his passport or facing arrest—perhaps, Judah suggests, because Serb authorities preferred that he keep "his militants in check."

So he did, until Kosovo Albanians recognized, after the sell-out at Dayton, that Washington understands only force. By then "a guerrilla cum terrorist organization called the [KLA] began to emerge in the province," rejecting Rugova's policies and "call[ing] for war on the Serbs" (Judah).

In an analysis of the origins, growth, and likely future of the KLA, Chris Hedges writes that it was founded in 1991, "its membership largely drawn from a few clans in Kosovo and radicals in the Albanian diaspora," and carried out its first armed attack in May 1993, killing two Serb police officers and wounding five.[14]

Hedges describes the organization as split "down a bizarre ideological divide, with hints of fascism on one side and whiffs of communism on the other. The former faction is led by...the heirs of those who fought in the World War II fascist militias and the Skandenbeg volunteer SS division raised by the Nazis, or the descendants of the rightist Albanian *kacak* rebels who rose up against the Serbs 80 years ago." "The second KLA faction, comprising most of the KLA leaders in exile, are old Stalinists who were once bankrolled by the xenophobic Enver Hoxha, the dictator of Albania who died in 1985." Hedges expected that the KLA would rule Kosovo after a NATO restoration by violence. He suggests further that the leadership may become "utterly disenchanted with the West—and as if they were not already implacable enough—turn to Islamic radicals ready to back another battle by Muslims against Orthodox Christians," noting "signs that contacts have been established." The sole doctrine the two KLA factions "agree on is the need to liberate Kosovo from Serbian rule. All else, menacingly, will be decided later. It is not said how." As Judah puts it, "the whip would change hands and pass to the 'enemy' community," as in the past, most recently under Nazi occupation, when the Albanian militias organized by the Nazis "indiscriminately killed Serbs and Montenegrins in Kosovo" and drove out tens of thousands (Vickers).

Current press reports indicate that factional splits remain deep, both within the KLA, and between the rising Albanian Kosovar leadership and the former Rugova parallel government. And of course the character of the conflict and the participants changed radically with the NATO military actions.[15]

Like other observers, Hedges reports that Kosovo Albanians felt "a deep, deep sense of betrayal" because of lack of Western support for their "peaceful, civilized protest," which was "ignored." And Dayton "taught us a painful truth, [that] those who want freedom must fight for it" (quoting a KLA commander). "As a result," Vickers writes, "the growing despair and frustration, noticeable by now among women and older people, allowed the passive policies of the Albanian resistance to be replaced by a more offensive strategy," manifested in "simultaneous bomb attacks on five camps housing Serb refugees in several towns throughout Kosovo in mid-February 1996." These were refugees driven from Croatia in the U.S.-authorized ethnic cleansing operations designed to set the stage for partition, the local architect appointed as the military commander of the KLA in May 1999.

Vickers reports that the guerrillas had become a substantial military force by the mid-'90s, with 40,000 soldiers in four regiments deployed in border regions of Kosovo and based in Albania. They were well-equipped with arms, funded by the wealthy Kosovar diaspora and perhaps militant Islamic groups in the Middle East, and trained in Albania, Iran, and Pakistan. From 1995 they increased their attacks on police stations and other targets, moving from sporadic killings to organized assaults. In April 1996, after killing several Serb policemen and civilians, the KLA officially announced that it had undertaken "an armed assault against Serbian aggressors" and that it was "operating a struggle for the liberation of Kosovo that would continue until complete independence." Attacks against Serb police and others, including alleged Albanian collaborators, continued through 1997. In December, the KLA made its first public appearance at the funeral of an Albanian teacher killed by Serb security forces. A spokesperson for the Republic of Kosovo observed on December 7 that the non-violent movement had been a complete failure:

> At a time when the international community has been underestimating and seriously ignoring the Albanian factor, reducing it to a problem of minorities requiring solutions in ridiculous frameworks with Serbia, when Serbia's only way of communicating with Albania is violence and crime, one should not be amazed if part of the people

decide to end this agony and take the fate of Kosovo and its people in its own hands.[16]

By February 1998, guerrilla operations reached much greater scale, as the KLA "not only fought Serbian Army and Interior Ministry police but also gunned down civilians, killing Serbian mail carriers and others associated with Belgrade."[17] These events elicited a much harsher Serbian military and police response, with brutal retaliation against civilians regarded as supporters of the KLA. Serbia interpreted the official U.S. government position as a "green light" for this reaction, Hedges suggests. In February 1998, U.S. Special Envoy to the Balkans Robert Gelbard had announced in Pristina that the U.S. regards the KLA as "without any question a terrorist group" and "condemns very strongly terrorist activities in Kosovo." Within two weeks, Serb forces brutally attacked the small town that was the headquarters of the Jashari clan "that made up much of the KLA at the start of the rebellion," turning it "into a smoldering ruin" with almost 100 people killed. That act "ignited the uprising."

The uprising was not anticipated by the KLA or the Serbs, Judah reports, though the KLA reacted quickly, distributing arms, forming militias, and determining to "fight the Serbs," now joined by many other Kosovo Albanians. Within months the KLA had occupied large areas of the province "while the Serbs, uncertain what to do, were not fighting back." When they did, in the summer of 1998, the KLA "melted into the hills as the Serbs wreaked their revenge by burning villages and driving out their people."[18] By the summer of 1998 the KLA had taken control of 40% of Kosovo, two *New York Times* reporters write in a lengthy review of the background, "and Mr. Milosevic responded with a major offensive," just as he was to react to the NATO bombing with "the expulsion, this time within weeks, of hundreds of thousands of people."[19]

We need scarcely tarry on how the U.S. would respond to attacks by a guerrilla force with foreign bases and supplies, seeking, say, independence for Puerto Rico, or reunification with Mexico of the southwest regions conquered by the expanding North American giant, taking control of 40% of the territory.

It is not hard to understand why the Serbian leadership might have interpreted Washington's official position as a "green light." They were fully aware of Washington's support for Croatian ethnic cleansing in Krajina. Judah suggests that the U.S. also gave a green light to the Serb attack on Srebrenica, which led to the slaughter of 7000 people, as part of a broader plan of population exchange. The U.S. did "nothing to prevent" the attack though it was aware of Serb preparations for it, and then used the Srebrenica massacre "to distract attention from the exodus of Krajina's entire population which was then taking place." Ethnic cleansing in Krajina was "simplifying matters," as Secretary of State Warren Christopher observed a year later.[20]

Serb leaders might also have had in mind the model of Lebanon, where the U.S. effectively authorized murderous Syrian attacks on Palestinians in 1976, and regular Israeli attacks on Palestinians and Lebanese before and since, often with a huge toll of deaths and refugees. These atrocities within Lebanon, which peaked under Nobel Peace Laureate Shimon Peres, are not an entirely appropriate analogue, however. From the mid-1980s until today these have typically been traceable to attacks on Israeli military forces occupying foreign territory in violation of long-standing Security Council orders to withdraw. Often such attacks make no pretense of retaliation. One air attack in December 1975, which killed over 50 people, was apparently in "retaliation" against the Security Council of the United Nations, then in session to consider a two-state settlement of the Israel-Palestine conflict, supported by virtually the entire world but vetoed by the U.S., hence vetoed from history along with a multitude of other events that depart from "the peace process." Israel's U.S.-backed 1982 invasion that devastated much of Lebanon and left 20,000 civilians dead was motivated by similar concerns, a matter familiar to Israeli scholarship and media, though a different story is preferred in the U.S.

The process continued into the 1990s, always with firm U.S. support. The most extreme examples have been under the Labor leadership that the U.S. has consistently preferred: Yitzhak Rabin's 1993 offensive that drove a half million people from their homes, and Peres's replay in 1996 with similar consequences, creating a "tremendous humanitarian crisis," the U.N. reported. That attack was halted only after the massacre of 100 refugees in the U.N. camp at Qana led to such strong international protest that the Clinton Administration had to withdraw its earlier justification for the atrocity.[21]

Note that these events of the mid-'90s give further insight into the operative values "when ethnic conflict turns into ethnic cleansing" (Clinton).

Returning to Kosovo, fighting escalated through 1998, the scale of atrocities corresponding roughly to the resources of violence. According to retrospectives in the *Washington Post*, "approximately 10,000 Interior troops fought the rebels and harassed and sometimes massacred civilians in rural rebel strongholds," and by the end of the year the army was also involved, according to unidentified NATO officials. By October, as U.S. envoy Richard Holbrooke reached an agreement with Milosevic (formal, and not observed), U.S. intelligence reported "that the Kosovo rebels intended to draw NATO into its fight for independence by provoking Serbian forces into further atrocities." A massacre in Racak on January 15, 1999, with some 45 civilians killed, received extensive coverage and is held to have been the decisive event that impelled Washington and its allies, horrified by the atrocity, to initiate preparations for war. "Racak transformed the West's Balkan policy as singular events seldom do," *Washington Post* correspondent Barton Gellman observed in reconstructing "the path to crisis." This was the "Defining Atrocity" that "Set Wheels in Motion." It "convinced the administration and then its NATO allies" that they must turn to war, soon initiating "a military campaign whose central objective was saving the lives and homes of Kosovo's ethnic Albanians" and that at once "greatly accelerated their slaughter and dispossession"—as predicted.[22]

There are simple ways to evaluate the plausibility of the contention that the Racak massacre had the described impact on Western sensibilities. We return to some of the more obvious tests.

An October 1998 cease-fire had made it possible to deploy 2000 OSCE monitors. Breakdown of U.S.-Milosevic negotiations led to renewed fighting and atrocities, which presumably increased with the threat of NATO bombing and the withdrawal of the monitors, again as predicted.[23] Officials of the U.N. refugee agency and Catholic Relief Services had warned that the threat of bombing "would imperil the lives of tens of thousands of refugees believed to be hiding in the woods," predicting "tragic" consequences if "NATO made it impossible for us to be here."[24]

Atrocities then sharply escalated after the March 24 bombing provided "motive and opportunity," as was surely "predictable," if not "entirely" so.

The anticipated consequences go well beyond the severe and immediate harm to Kosovo Albanians. Among them are death and destruction throughout the FRY. One instructive example is Vojvodina, at once attacked with extreme severity, particularly its capital city Novi Sad, where bridges, infrastructure, water supplies and electricity were quickly devastated. The home of the Hungarian minority, Vojvodina is hundreds of miles from Kosovo and was a peaceful region until NATO bombed. Just days before the bombing there were no signs of conflict or disruption according to highly credible observers who passed through, having been ordered by international organizations to leave Yugoslavia.[25]

The province had been "a symbol of resistance to Slobodan Milosevic's regime," the press reports, "a place where opposition political leaders spoke of Western-style reform, where ethnic minorities lived in harmony, and where much of the population favored greater autonomy from Belgrade." But having instantly "become a ground zero in NATO's bombing campaign against Yugoslavia,...nearly all pro-Western sentiment has been crushed." "The democratic opposition in Vojvodina—once a bright spot in Yugoslavia's otherwise dismal political scene—has become a vociferous enemy of NATO." An executive board member of the Novi Sad City Council, a leader of "a progressive opposition party," observes that "NATO showed they only understand the policy of violence." He concludes that Vojvodina, the country's agricultural center and source of nearly half of its gross domestic product in 1998, is being "struck so frequently to destroy the Serbian economy." The first two bridges that were destroyed "were favorite walking bridges for the people of Novi Sad." They "had no military uses," he says: one "was barely strong enough to support buses" and the other connected Novi Sad to a small village and was not a main transportation link. Within a few weeks water supplies were destroyed and electricity largely so, along with much of the health system and, it was feared, import of medicines and veterinary drugs. Forced "to concentrate on issues of daily survival," people were not "moving to press the Government to yield to NATO's conditions," a predictable consequence that is not problematic if the goal is to devastate the society.[26]

Independent sources (see note 25) report that opposition centers in central Serbia (Nis, Kragujevac, Cacak, Valjevo) were the most severely damaged by the bombing. Nis mayor Zoran Zivkovic, deputy leader of the Democratic Party, strongly condemned Milosevic and his disastrous policy. The independent Beta News Agency (Yugoslav, but not state-run like Tanjug) reported an estimate by Vojvodina authorities in early June that the NATO bombing damage had reached the level of about $4.8 billion, including the destruction of 3650 housing facilities and eighty-two enterprises damaged or completely destroyed. The statistics were transmitted by Serb authorities and have to be regarded with skepticism, but there is little doubt about the general picture.

The undermining of the democratic opposition in the Federal Republic of Yugoslavia generally, not only Vojvodina, was another consequence of the NATO bombing, also surely anticipated. We return to this and other consequences, and the differing reactions in the enlightened states and beyond.

Quite naturally, U.S. propaganda, and that of its allies, makes every effort to divert attention from the conclusions that might be drawn by attending to the consequences of the resort to force. One method is to strike poses of nobility and humanitarian passion, with the expectation, amply fulfilled, that they will be echoed in a drumbeat of appropriate rhetoric. Another is the claim that the atrocities were going to happen anyway, as proven by the meticulous planning with which they were executed after the bombing: *Operation Horseshoe*, allegedly discovered well after the results of the bombing were evident. We return to the most detailed evidence offered by official sources. However, without any information about *Operation Horseshoe*, we can be confident that Serbia had such plans. The brief historical review makes that clear enough, and suffices to explain why. Even living in total peace and security, the U.S. has innumerable contingency plans for actions ranging from nuclear destruction (first-strike targeting Third World non-nuclear states remains official U.S. policy; see chap. 6, below) to lesser actions. Perhaps the U.S. has contingency plans even to invade Canada.[27] If not, it would design and implement them quickly enough, and not very politely, were Canada to bomb Washington; Canada could not then claim very plausibly that it was going to happen anyway. That Milosevic had plans to drive the Albanian population out of Serbia is vastly more likely in the light of his well-known record, the history of Albanian-Serbian relations in Kosovo, and U.S. threats. If NATO had no inkling of this, it would be remarkable indeed.

The culpability of Clinton, Blair, and their associates would pass beyond astonishing ignorance to extreme criminality if indeed they knew (as they now claim) that huge atrocities were underway or about to occur while doing nothing whatsoever to prepare for the flood of refugees they anticipated. And the criminality mounts still higher if they failed to notify Commanding General Clark, as he maintains. A month after the bombing began General Clark reported that the plans for *Operation Horseshoe* "have never been shared with me," and—even more incriminating—that the NATO operation planned by "the political leadership"

> was not designed as a means of blocking Serb ethnic cleansing. It was not designed as a means of waging war against the Serb and MUP forces in Kosovo. Not in any way. There was never any intent to do that. That was not the idea.[28]

The Commanding General, in short, regarded the ethnic cleansing operations of Serbia as "entirely predictable" and "not in any way" a concern of the political leadership who ordered the bombing that evoked the atrocities: doubtless an exaggeration, but close enough to the mark to allow reasonable people to draw some conclusions.

The agency that bears primary responsibility for care of refugees is the U.N.'s UNHCR (see p. 16). In October 1998, the UNHCR announced that by January 1999 it would have to eliminate a fifth of its staff because of a budgetary crisis, with a decline of over 15% in 1998. This is part of the general budgetary crisis of the U.N., resulting primarily from the refusal of the U.S. to pay its debt, one of its many violations of treaty obligations, particularly in the era of the New Humanism, matters to which we return. The announcement of the sharp cutbacks in staff for refugee care coincided with Clinton's expression of great concern about refugees who would have to face the bitter winter in Kosovo, and with the U.S./British announcement that they believe they have "sufficient authority to launch air strikes" on the basis of Security Council resolutions and a report by the Secretary-General, military actions that would surely exacerbate the refugee crisis.[29]

The configuration of events lends further insight into the "principles and values" that inspire soulful acclamations.

CHAPTER 3

Assessing Humanitarian Intent

The events in Kosovo alone suffice to eliminate from consideration the primary and most exalted argument for the resort to force: that the NATO bombings, undertaken with humanitarian intent, open a new era in which the reigning superpower and its junior partner, suffused with previously-undetectable nobility, promise to lead the way to a new era of humanism and justice.

Apart from the evidence from the Balkans, there are elementary ways to test the thesis that is pronounced with such authority and solemnity: ask how the same enlightened states behave elsewhere. True, that requires breaking the rule that attention be restricted to the crimes of official enemies. But let us allow ourselves that lapse, still keeping, however, to another central principle: the past cannot be permitted to confuse the discussion, the familiar doctrine of "change of course." The current variant is that we must exclude anything that took place during the Cold War, when there were (understandable) mistakes and errors. Illustrations of this doctrine are too numerous to mention.[1]

Why the doctrine must be upheld with such rigor will quickly be discovered by anyone who departs from it—discovering, for example, that crimes of the Cold War had little or nothing to do with the conflict, as sometimes acknowledged in high-level internal discussion, and that the systematic pattern precedes and follows the Cold War with little change apart from public rationale and effects of the disappearance of a deterrent.[2]

Let us nonetheless adhere to the doctrine while departing from the second leading principle: that we focus laser-like on crimes of selected enemies, at the moment Serbian devils. This departure has at least two merits: (1) it allows us to test the New Humanism, and (2) we can attend to issues that are of more importance on any moral scale.

Perhaps it is worthwhile to digress briefly to mention a few truisms. The first is that people are primarily responsible for the likely consequences of their own actions, or inaction. The second is that the concern for moral issues (crimes, etc.) should vary in accordance with ability to have an effect (though that is of course not the only factor). A corollary is that responsibility mounts the greater the opportunities, and the more free one is to act without serious cost. Accordingly, responsibility is far greater for privileged people in more free societies than for those lacking privilege or facing severe penalties for honesty and moral integrity.

The two truisms tend to correlate, even coincide, yielding conclusions that a moral agent will draw in real-world cases, taking into account as well the corollary.

We understand these truisms very well at long range. Thus no one was impressed when Soviet commissars railed about U.S. crimes, even if they happened to be right and the crimes were serious or monstrous. We were much impressed, however, when dissidents condemned Soviet crimes, even lesser ones. The reasons are straightforward, the two moral truisms just mentioned—which, as is commonly the case, coincided in their implications. The corollary also holds: the commissars could at least plead fear in extenuation, not merely the advantages that accrue to subordination to power.

It is also useful to recall a psychological truism. One of the hardest things to do is to look into the mirror. It is also one of the most important things to do, because of the moral truisms. And there are powerful institutions that seek to protect people from engaging in this difficult and critically important task.

It may also be worthwhile to recall other truisms. Deploring the crimes of others often gives us a nice warm feeling: we are good people, so different from those bad people. That is particularly true when there is nothing much we can do about the crimes of others, so that we can strike impressive poses without cost to ourselves. Looking at our own crimes is much harder, and for those willing to do it, often carries costs. Every society has its "dissidents" and its "commissars," and it is close to a historical law that the commissars are highly praised and the dissidents bitterly condemned—within the society, that is; for official enemies the values are reversed. The costs of dissidence can be severe, notably in U.S. client states: the murdered Jesuit intellectuals in El Salvador, for example. A useful experiment is to ask products of an elite education to recall the names of the assassinated dissidents, or their writings, and then to compare the results with the same questions concerning Soviet dissidents, who were not treated anywhere near as harshly in the post-Stalin period. Equally instructive is inspection of the published record: reviews, books, articles in major intellectual journals, and so on. Such exercises in looking in the mirror can teach useful lessons—about ourselves, about our institutions.

These are matters that have been frequently discussed. They are so trivial that it may seem pointless to reiterate them. But perhaps it is useful nonetheless, particularly because the truisms are so commonly forgotten, and so easily illustrated. In the present case, for example.

3.1 The Racak Massacre:
"Defining Atrocity Set Wheels in Motion"

Let us begin with a minor example: a test of the thesis that the Racak massacre so offended the sensibilities of the leaders of the Free World that they had to prepare for war. We can both test the thesis, and observe the moral truisms, by asking how the same leaders have reacted to similar or worse massacres at the same time, where their own direct responsibility is enormous, and it would be unnecessary to resort to war, even threats, to mitigate or terminate terrible crimes.

The Racak massacre was reported by U.S. diplomat William Walker, leading his OSCE war crimes verification team to Racak. "From what I saw," he said, "I do not hesitate to describe the crime as a massacre, a crime against humanity. Nor do I hesitate to accuse the government security forces of responsibility."[3] Let us accept his conclusions as completely accurate.[4] We may note further that Walker is an expert in verifying state crimes. He served as U.S. Ambassador to El Salvador, where he administered the U.S. support that allowed the government to carry out extreme state terror, peaking once again in November 1989 in an outburst of violence that included the murder of six leading Salvadoran dissident intellectuals, Jesuit priests, along with their housekeeper and her daughter. Their brains were blown out by the U.S.-trained Atlacatl brigade, which had compiled a remarkable record of shocking acts. These were much the same hands, with the same guidance, that had murdered Archbishop Romero to open the terrible decade of U.S.-guided atrocities in El Salvador, in large measure a war against the Church, which had violated the norms of good behavior and infuriated the leading enlightened state by adopting "the preferential option for the poor."

Walker was as quick to respond to the murder of the Jesuit intellectuals as he was to the Racak massacre. He supervised the intimidation of the main eyewitness by the U.S. Embassy and its Salvadoran client, who naturally sought to discredit her testimony (withdrawn under pressure). He then "told congressional investigators there was no evidence to implicate the military and hypothesized that leftist rebels might have committed the act while dressed in soldiers' garb," Americas Watch reported in disgust. Walker's efforts to deny the atrocities carried out by Washington's client killers came "long after a Salvadoran colonel had told a U.S. major that the Army had committed the murders," Americas Watch continued, reviewing his efforts to evade the obvious. He then recommended to Secretary of State James Baker that the U.S. "not jeopardize" its relationship with El Salvador by investigating "past deaths, however heinous"—a wise decision, given the decisive U.S. role in the atrocities, including his own.[5]

In January 1999, Walker received great praise for his heroism at Racak, inspired by his recognition that he "may not have done enough to stop past atrocities" (Ted Koppel, *Nightline*) and by his regret for his "silence" on the assassination of the Jesuits, when he was "speechless" (*Washington Post*). We await his heroic denunciations of Washington's crimes.[6]

"These two events—the murder of Archbishop Romero in 1980 and the slaying of the Jesuits in 1989—stand as bookends to the decade offering harsh testimony about who really rules El Salvador and how little they have changed," Americas Watch observed in its review of the year of Walker's service to the cause. "Ten years later, priest-killing is still a preferred option for those who simply will not hear the cries for change and justice in a society that has had too little of either." The Jesuit intellectuals joined a long list of religious martyrs, and hundreds of thousands of other victims of the reign of terror organized and directed by Washington in that grim decade.

We should be permitted to recall at least the second of the "bookends to the decade," which is just within the designated time frame for the onset of the New Humanism, coinciding with the fall of the Berlin Wall, the event that at last released the two enlightened states from the Cold War antagonisms that had hampered their dedication to justice, freedom, and human rights generally.

Let us move on to a decade later, still seeking to evaluate the thesis that it was their horror over the Racak massacre that impelled the enlightened states to war.

Consider East Timor, the site of the worst slaughter relative to population since the Holocaust, it appears, thanks to the support of the U.S. and U.K. (helped by others, to be sure), including diplomatic support, crucial military aid, and equally crucial falsification and denial. It should be unnecessary to review the facts, carefully suppressed during the worst days of the slaughter (when terminating it would have been simple and costless), and still often denied.[7] But the doctrine of "change of course," to which we have agreed to adhere, renders such review irrelevant in any event, so let us keep to 1999.

After 25 years of horror, steps were finally taken that might permit the tortured people of the territory to exercise the right of self-determination that has been upheld by the U.N. Security Council and the International Court of Justice. The Indonesian government agreed to permit a referendum in August 1999, in which Timorese are to be permitted to choose or reject "autonomy" within Indonesia. It is taken for granted on all sides that if the vote is minimally free, pro-independence forces will win. The occupying Indonesian army (ABRI/TNI) moved at once to prevent this outcome. The primary device was to organize paramilitary forces to kill, torture, and terrorize while ABRI adopted the stance of "plausible deniability," which quickly collapsed in the presence of foreign observers (including Australian journalists, the Irish Foreign Minister, aid workers, etc.), who could see firsthand that ABRI was arming and guiding the killers, and allowing them free rein.

In April 1999 alone over 100 people were reported to have been massacred, more than twice the number in Racak, including some 60 people murdered in a church in Liquica on April 6 according to the figures provided by the Foundation for Legal and Human Rights in the capital city of Dili, which listed names. They were among thousands fleeing from terrorist rampages, finally taking refuge in the church, which was attacked by soldiers and paramilitaries whose aim "was to murder all the people in the church," the parish priest wrote in a local journal.

Eighteen more were murdered in the town of Suai from April 9 to 14 along with ten tortured and nine disappeared, according to the Church-based Peace and Justice Commission. Church, human rights, and women's groups reported that hundreds were "killed and wounded" in these attacks. After villagers "pulled rotting corpses from the ocean on April 24, human rights workers said the death toll from the Suai massacres alone might top 100." A few days later militia attacks left "at least 30 dead" in Dili (April 16–17), along with "dozens abducted and possibly executed," the Australian press reported under the lead headline "Freedom Slaughtered." Thousands of others were herded into Indonesian concentration camps, perhaps 10,000 in one camp on the outskirts of Liquica where conditions were reported to be desperate and humiliating. Tens of thousands of others fled the countryside in terror. The Dili office of the Catholic Relief Agency Caritas warned staff that they would be attacked if they tried to provide food to refugees. Australian aid workers had been forced to flee in February. U.S. doctor Dan Murphy, a volunteer in Dili (later forced out of the country for several weeks), reported that fifty to 100 Timorese are dying daily from curable diseases while Indonesia "had a deliberate policy not to allow medical supplies into East Timor." As of early June, Indonesian authorities were still barring an Australian medical team from entering "to ease an unfolding humanitarian disaster."[8]

ABRI's militias are "well-organised death squads, unleashed by a hidden, or partly hidden, hand—the public expression of a private and calculated intelligence." Australia's leading specialist on the Indonesian army describes the militias as "fundamentally an extension of the TNI [ABRI]," secretly organized in October 1998 "to wage a proxy war on the army's behalf against the independence forces."[9]

"The population of East Timor is crying out for help but has been abandoned by the international community yet again," Australian commentator Andrew McNaughtan observed—accurately. But not for lack of information. Meeting in the wake of the "bloody rampage" in Dili in mid-April, the U.N. Security Council heard a report from its special envoy on East Timor, leading to calls for pressure on Indonesia to call off the violence, from Brazil and Japan (which has traditionally been highly supportive of the Indonesian government). Some U.N. observers finally entered in May to monitor the upcoming referendum, but Jakarta refused to allow them to carry arms, even handguns for protection, insisting that "its 17,000 strong security force will remain responsible for security" in the illegally annexed province.[10]

How have the guardians of virtue responded to the latest stages of the Indonesian atrocities that they have long supported? New Labor took office with an "ethical foreign policy" under the guidance of Robin Cook, who announced that "we have made a firm commitment not to permit the sale of arms to regimes that might use them for repression or aggression." But "He will not block the sale of armoured vehicles to a regime which has one of the worst human rights records, sources say." His government at once stepped up arms sales to

Indonesia, granting fifty-six military export licences while he "acknowledged that British equipment was being used against demonstrators" of Indonesia's democracy movement. "Broad categories cleared for export included small arms, machine guns, bombs, riot control and toxicological agents, surveillance systems, 'armoured goods', electronic equipment specially designed for military use, and aircraft"; the government also completed delivery of Hawk all-weather attack fighters, more expected. "Labour is exporting more guns and other military equipment to Indonesia than the Tories—in spite of Robin Cook's much-vaunted 'ethical' foreign policy," the press reported, while "sales of small arms, including machineguns, have even doubled under Labour." In justification, the Foreign Office cited improvements in the situation in East Timor. British armaments are used to crush dissent in East Timor, the Indonesian Defense attaché reported on British TV, as in Indonesia itself. Arms manufacturers "are more likely to have their export licences approved under Labour than they were under the Tories," John Pilger reports: "Fewer than one per cent of applications were turned down" during Labour's first year in office." An ethical foreign policy is fine, correspondent Hugh O'Shaugnessy observed, but "No, Minister, British Aerospace cannot do without Indonesian business"; like Pilger, he has covered Timor and other areas with great distinction. As for the U.S., Clinton has signed congressional legislation banning the use of U.S. weapons in East Timor, and education and training of ABRI. But without careful monitoring his signature is worthless, as proven in the past when he used various devices to evade congressional restrictions on training of Indonesian military officers, causing much irritation in Congress but little notice elsewhere.[11]

No call has been heard from the New Humanists for withdrawal of Indonesian military forces or for sending a meaningful U.N. observer force. Quite the contrary. They appear to be impeding the dispatch of such a force, so we learn from Farhan Haq of the Inter Press Service (IPS), reporting from the United Nations in New York under the headline: "Politics—East Timor: U.S. Delays Arrival of U.N. Police Monitors." "The U.N.'s hopes of quickly deploying police monitors in increasingly volatile East Timor have hit a new snag, with President Bill Clinton forced to delay U.S. approval until he consults Congress." U.N. officials "had planned to have slightly more than 270 police officers in place by the end of June," but Clinton's hands are tied by a 1993 directive he issued "in the aftermath of Washington's bungled involvement in a U.N. mission in Somalia," which "likely will delay approval of the police" and in turn "complicate the entire voting timetable, say U.N. officials."[12]

Francesco Vendrell, the U.N. Diplomat who heads the Asia/Pacific Division of the U.N. Department for Political Affairs and has been working for a peaceful reversal of the aggression for twenty-five years, says that "there is a draft resolution in place" for Council approval of the police, but it cannot be enacted without U.S. authorization, and Clinton must still "give two weeks' notice to Congress before it can approve the deployment of the U.N. Mission." Unlike the War Powers Act, this directive must be observed. At the time of writing, it is unclear whether notice has even been given, though the issue has been on the agenda for months as atrocities mounted, organized by the murderous military forces of the long-time ally of Washington/London. The U.N. accord calling for a referendum and monitors was signed on May 5, twenty-three days before IPS reported that Clinton had still failed to give the required two-week notice to Congress. Coverage in the U.S. is so scanty and superficial that any comment has to be tentative, and the facts will probably emerge only much later, the usual state of affairs with regard to atrocities acceptable to, or traceable to, the New Humanism.

"Time is of the essence for East Timor," Vendrell and other U.N. officials point out. Voter registration was to begin by about June 20. "'Every day lost is a real danger to the whole consultation process,' says Sidney Jones, executive director of Human Rights Watch/Asia." The possibility of a meaningful vote might already have been successfully undermined by Indonesian terror, which had driven leaders underground or abroad while "some 35,000 Timorese have been driven from their homes to camps patrolled by pro-Indonesia forces."[13]

The small U.N. contingent did attempt to investigate new atrocities in late May, reporting that paramilitaries had attacked the hamlet of Atara, killing at least six people preparing to go to church on Sunday morning—perhaps five times that many, local human rights groups allege. The U.N. investigators were prevented from reaching Atara, but they did report that they had "stumbled across preparations for further attacks" by the same forces, a military camp where they were being trained by ABRI in clear violation of the U.N. accord signed by Indonesia.[14]

In its assessment in late May, the "respected human rights group" Foundation for Legal and Human Rights in Dili described the "atmosphere of fear" as the worst since the period from 1975 to 1989, "when the violence-racked territory was closed to foreigners." "Every day has been marked with violence, kidnapping, torture, killing, looting and arson directed towards East Timorese throughout the territory," the Foundation reported.[15]

The New Humanists have exerted no pressures on Indonesia, as far as is known, apart from alleged critical words in private and a few taps on the wrist. Racak is a serious matter, not to be confused with yet another episode in a long horror story that has proceeded with decisive U.S./British support. From this example alone—one of many—it follows that we cannot take seriously the display of outrage over Racak, let alone the claim that moral indignation over this "defining atrocity" impelled those who are "upholding our values" to turn to force.

True, this conclusion violates a significant precept of the New Humanism, as of the old, articulated lucidly by former *New York Times* correspondent A.J. Langguth, expressing his irritation at the first extensive discussion of the U.S.-backed Indonesian slaughter in East Timor after several years of government and press fabrication, then total—literally, *total*—silence as violent ethnic cleansing and atrocities peaked in 1977–78, reaching levels that many consider genocidal, with a death toll of perhaps 200,000, over a quarter of the population. He objected, quite accurately, that "if the world were to converge suddenly on Timor, it wouldn't improve the lot of a single Cambodian." At the time, the mission was to contribute to the huge outpouring of moral outrage over the crimes of the Khmer Rouge, a task that had a number of merits: the immediate agent was an official enemy; there was no hint of a suggestion as to how the crimes could be mitigated (in dramatic contrast to Timor and other major atrocities at the same time); these massive crimes could be used to provide a retrospective justification for even greater crimes committed by the U.S. in its wars in Indochina; and perhaps most important of all, the crimes could be invoked to justify ongoing and projected crimes on grounds that they would deter "the Pol Pot left"—priests and peasants in El Salvador, for example. In this context, Langguth's objection was appropriate: attention to huge crimes conducted with decisive U.S. participation is an improper distraction.[16]

The argument is entirely rational on the reigning doctrinal principles, and has been reiterated forcefully throughout the Kosovo conflict in response to the observation that any serious assessment of the self-congratulatory rhetoric will ask how the New Humanists behave when faced, at the very same time, with comparable or worse atrocities that they could reduce or terminate easily and costlessly, merely by withdrawing their participation in them. In these cases too, attention to U.S./U.K crimes "wouldn't improve the lot of a single Kosovo Albanian," and therefore is a proper object of derision and scorn.

Let us nevertheless pursue this course in a further effort to evaluate the self-description of the New Humanists, recognizing—despite the indignation it provokes—that this is an elementary prerequisite for inquiry into their motives and goals, and the implications for the future.

3.2 Humanitarian Concerns in the '90s: A Small Sample

Before proceeding, we might take note of a simple point of logic. When a humanitarian crisis develops, outsiders have three choices:

(I) act to escalate the catastrophe

(II) do nothing

(III) try to mitigate the catastrophe

Kosovo falls under category (I), East Timor in 1999 under (II)—a particularly ugly example given the very recent history that is off the record under the doctrine of "change of course." Let us consider some other current examples.

One instructive case is Colombia, through the 1990s the scene of the worst humanitarian crisis in the Western hemisphere—not so much because the crisis became sharply worse, but because U.S.-run slaughters and terror in Central America in the preceding years had largely achieved their goals, and other means became available to maintain order as a result of the economic catastrophe of the 1980s and opportunities afforded by the changed international economy.

Recall that in Kosovo Western sources estimated 2000 killed on both sides in the year prior to the bombing, and perhaps 2–300,000 internal refugees. As the bombing began, the State Department released its report for Colombia during the same year. The figures are eerily similar: 2–3000 killed, 300,000 new refugees, about 80% of massacres (where there is credible evidence) attributed to paramilitaries and the military, who, for years, have used the paras approximately as ABRI does in East Timor and the Serb military did in Kosovo.[17]

No two historical examples are quite parallel, of course. There are differences between Colombia and Kosovo, two of them particularly significant.

First, in Colombia these atrocities are not new (as in Kosovo from early 1998, according to NATO and the scholarly literature). Rather, they are added to an annual toll that has been much the same. The State Department gave similar estimates in its report for 1997, as have human rights monitors for many years.[18] In 1998, according to the State Department, the refugee flow even surpassed that of earlier years. The refugee total is estimated by Church and other human rights groups at well over a million, mostly women and children, one of the worst refugee crises in the world. In 1998 the situation deteriorated to such an extent that one of Colombia's most prominent and courageous human rights activists, Father Javier Giraldo, who heads the Church-based Peace and Justice Center, had to flee the country under death threats, joining many others. A year earlier, Amnesty International had selected Colombia as the first site for a global campaign for protection of human rights monitors, a natural choice in the light of the record.[19]

Like AI, Human Rights Watch, Church-based groups, and other organizations concerned with human rights, the State Department concludes that "credible allegations of cooperation [of the armed forces] with paramilitary groups, including instances of both silent support and direct collaboration by members of the armed forces, in particular the army, continued" through 1998: "There were tacit arrangements between local military commanders and paramilitary groups in some regions, and paramilitary groups operated freely in some areas that were under military control." Other reports are far more detailed, but with the same essential conclusion about the paramilitaries: many of their killings are "carried out with the tolerance or active participation of the security forces," Human Rights Watch reports once again in October 1998.

The second difference is that in this case the blood is on Washington's hands. The state terror operations follow guidelines provided by the Kennedy Administration, which advised the Colombian military to "select civilian and military personnel... [to]...as necessary execute paramilitary, sabotage and/or terrorist activities against known Communist proponents. It should be backed by the United States." Citing these doctrines, Human Rights Watch points out that "known Communist proponents" include "government critics, trade unionists, community organizers, opposition politicians, civic leaders, and human rights activists," as social protest was officially labelled "the unarmed branch of subversion."[20] The sole independent political party was virtually eliminated by assassination of thousands of its elected officials, candidates, and activists. The primary victims have been peasants, particularly those who dared to raise their heads in a regime of brutal repression and enormous poverty in the midst of highly-praised economic success (for domestic elites and foreign investors).

Colombia became the leading Western Hemisphere recipient of U.S. arms and training as violence increased through the '90s. The Clinton administration was particularly enthusiastic in its praise for President Gavíria, whose tenure in office was responsible for "appalling levels of violence," according to the major human rights organizations, even surpassing his predecessors as "violence reached unprecedented levels." Atrocities run the gamut. Currently U.S.

military aid continues to be "used in indiscriminate bombing" and other atrocities, and is slated to increase sharply for 1999, probably taking first place internationally (apart from Israel and Egypt, which belong to a separate category). The aid is provided under a "drug war" pretext that is dismissed by almost all serious observers.[21]

The example provides a current illustration of option (I): act to escalate the atrocities, as in Kosovo—as systematically in the past in a long series of cases that are barred from inspection by the doctrine of "change of course."

The humanitarian crisis in Kosovo, of course, passed far beyond the level of Colombia after the NATO bombing began: "the result" that was "entirely predictable," or at least plausibly anticipated, according to high-level U.S. sources. Two months later, as noted, refugee flight to neighboring countries and destruction of villages had reached the level of Palestine 1948, in addition to hundreds of thousands of new internal refugees and atrocities that greatly exceed those of 1948 (which were serious enough), on a scale as yet unknown though they are certain to be extensively investigated and publicized, unlike others that are comparable or worse but are attributable to the wrong source.[22]

The next reasonable step in evaluating the New Humanism would be to ask how it responds to atrocities of the 1990s that are on the scale of the anticipated results of the resort to bombing in Kosovo, keeping to cases where the enlightened states could readily act to mitigate or terminate such humanitarian catastrophes. That step too turns out to be straightforward.

In announcing the "new internationalism where the brutal repression of whole ethnic groups will no longer be tolerated," Tony Blair also declared—somewhat more plausibly—that "On its 50th birthday NATO must prevail."[23] The anniversary of NATO was celebrated in Washington in April 1999, a grim commemoration in the shadow of the ethnic cleansing that was proceeding in Kosovo, not far from NATO's borders. The anniversary meetings were widely reported. It required impressive discipline for participants and commentators "not to notice" that some of the worst ethnic cleansing of the '90s, well beyond what had been attributed to Milosevic in Kosovo, was taking place within NATO itself, and within the jurisdiction of the Council of Europe and the European Court of Human Rights, which regularly issues judgments finding NATO member Turkey "responsible for burning villages, inhuman and degrading treatment, and appalling failures to investigate allegations of ill-treatment at the hands of the security forces."[24] Turkey has not been formally accepted as a member of the European Union because of its human rights record, which has disturbed some Europeans, unlike Washington, "which happens to support Turkish membership."[25] Looking at that forbidden topic, we find that after the NATO bombing, atrocities in Kosovo escalated from the level of (Clinton-backed) atrocities in the Western Hemisphere to a scale that might compare with that of (Clinton-backed) ethnic cleansing within NATO itself.

For many years, Turkish repression of Kurds has been a major scandal,[26] reaching even to criminalization of use of the Kurdish language or reference to Kurd identity. Anti-Kurdish repression was so extreme that even the law banning the language did not mention the word "Kurdish," referring only to "the use of languages other than Turkish." While that law was repealed in 1989, severe restrictions continue in effect. Kurdish radio and TV remain illegal, Kurdish may not be taught in schools or used in advertising, parents cannot give children Kurdish names, and so on. Violators are severely punished in Turkish prisons, often hardly more than torture chambers. In one notorious case, Turkish sociologist Dr. Ismail Besikci, who had already served fifteen years in jail for defending Kurdish rights, was arrested and imprisoned in 1991 for having published a book (*State Terror in the Near East*) exposing the government's treatment of Kurds.[27]

Defenders of the Turkish regime point out accurately that individual Kurds can integrate into Turkish society, on condition that they renounce any Kurdish identity.

In 1984 the Kurdish Workers Party (PKK), led by Abdullah Ocalan, initiated an armed struggle. Conflict continued through the 1980s, but Turkish military actions, along with repression and terror (closing newspapers and murdering journalists, and so on), increased sharply in 1991–2 with the dispatch of Black Hawk helicopters and other advanced U.S. military equipment. In March

1992 Ocalan announced a cease-fire after discussions with the Turgut Ozal government, which regarded the offer as "a genuine peace move." The cease-fire was renewed by the PKK in April, with the demand that Kurds "should be given our cultural freedoms and the right to broadcast in Kurdish," along with lifting of repressive "emergency legislation" and abolition of the "village guard system." Under this standard principle of counterinsurgency doctrine, applied in Guatemala and elsewhere, villagers are mobilized to "defend" their communities against guerrilla forces; or else.

Shortly after, President Ozal died. He "left two legacies on the Kurdish question itself," Tirman observes: "a small opening for politicians to cope more realistically with the fact of Kurdish grievances, and a military strategy that relied on overwhelming force in the Southeast and deportation of Kurds from their homelands. The second legacy was more durable," thanks in large measure to the preferences of the reigning superpower, which rushed sophisticated equipment to the Turkish military (jet planes, missiles, land-mine dispensers, etc.) so that it could escalate the ethnic cleansing and terror. "Turkish officers educated in the United States employed the methods familiar to peasants from Vietnam to Guatemala,"[28] where ethnic cleansing, massacre, terror and torture and other atrocities were carried out by U.S. clients, or in the worst cases, by U.S. armed forces directly. The doctrines were borrowed directly from the Nazis, then refined for application in U.S.-run counterinsurgency operations worldwide.[29]

But the instructions are to learn nothing from this history, so let us keep to the permitted time span: the 1990s.

Savage atrocities rapidly increased through the early '90s, peaking in 1994–96. One index is the flight of over a million Kurds from the countryside to the unofficial Kurdish capital Diyarbakir from 1990 to 1994, as the Turkish army was devastating the Southeast regions of heavy Kurdish settlement. The forced mass migration is reported to have swelled the population of Diyarbakir by over a million more in the two years that followed.[30] In 1994, the Turkish State Minister for Human Rights reported:

> The terror in Tunceli is state terror. The state has evacuated and
> burnt down villages in Tunceli. We insist on Tunceli. There are two
> million homeless people in the south-east. We cannot even give
> them a tent.[31]

The toll of internal refugees has increased substantially since, perhaps to 2.5 or 3 million, along with unknown numbers who have
fled the country. "Mystery killings" of Kurds alone (assumed to be
death squad killings) amounted to 3200 in 1993 and 1994. These
continued along with torture, destruction of some 3500 villages
(seven times Kosovo according to Clinton's figures), bombing with
napalm, and casualties generally estimated in the tens of thousands;
no one was counting.

In one particularly gruesome "ferocious campaign of village
destruction," Turkish military forces "demolished in the autumn of
1994 some 137 villages in the province of Tunceli, fully one-third
of all the villages in this large area north of Dyarbakir. Vast tracts of
fires in one of the last green areas of Turkey were set aflame from
[U.S.-supplied] helicopters and F-16s" (Tirman).

The killings are attributed to Kurdish terror in Turkish propaganda, generally adopted in the U.S. as well. The same practice is
followed in Colombia, and routinely by Serbian propaganda as well.
Like virtually all propaganda, these exercises have a measure of
truth. It would be hard, probably impossible, to find a war of aggression, imperial violence, or internal repression and slaughter that is
free of atrocities by the "terrorists" or "resistance" (depending on
the stance adopted); and equally hard to find a conflict of this
nature that is not rooted in the "silent violence" of socioeconomic,
cultural, and political arrangements imposed by force.

1994 marked two records in Turkey, veteran *Washington Post* correspondent Jonathan Randal reported from the scene: it was "the
year of the worst repression in the Kurdish provinces," and the year
when Turkey became "the biggest single importer of American military hardware and thus the world's largest arms purchaser. Its arse-
nal, 80 percent American, included M-60 tanks, F-16 fighter-
bombers, Cobra gunships, and Blackhawk 'slick' helicopters, all of
which were eventually used against the Kurds." U.S. firms are
involved in extensive co-production arrangements with Turkish

military industry. U.S. taxpayers have also paid tens of millions of dollars to train Turkish forces to fight Kurds, arms specialist William Hartung estimates. When human rights groups exposed Turkey's use of U.S. jets to bomb villages, the Clinton Administration found ways to evade laws requiring suspension of arms deliveries, much as it was doing in Indonesia and elsewhere.[32]

"The U.S. pours sophisticated weapons into Turkey's arsenals every year," Human Rights Watch reported in 1995, "becoming complicit in a scorched earth campaign that violates the fundamental tenets of international law." Its reports detail atrocities of the kind familiar from the front pages of every newspaper (concerning Kosovo), and many that are qualitatively different, since Turkey can freely use U.S. jets, helicopters, tanks, and other advanced weapons of destruction and massacre.[33] In addition to the usual methods of torture, assassination, and ethnic cleansing, the records reveal such actions as throwing people from helicopters (sometimes prisoners, sometimes abused women forced to strip naked before being thrown to their deaths), burning civilians alive while bound and tied with electric cables and chains, and a long and gory list of others. Courageous Turkish human rights activists have sought to report abuses, and have suffered for it. Members of the Human Rights Association "have been prosecuted, tortured, imprisoned and sometimes killed," and the Diyarbakir office was raided and closed in 1997, curtailing still further the reporting of human rights abuses.[34]

"Ferocious battles" continued through 1996–97, Tirman reports. "The war against the Kurds was very much alive" in 1997 when he wrote, in fact intensified after retraction of "flimsy comments about a political settlement." In 1999 the government is reported to have 300,000 forces deployed in the region, continuing the war. But successful state terror and ethnic cleansing have reduced the level of necessary atrocities below that of the mid-1990s, so Turkey is no longer the leading recipient of U.S. military aid (after the perennials: Israel and Egypt), displaced by Colombia.[35]

Turkish aircraft (i.e., U.S. aircraft with Turkish pilots) shifted to bombing Serbia, though correspondents report Turkish "fears that supporting independence for Albanian Kosovars could encourage

Kurdish separatism within its own borders." Meanwhile Turkey is lauded for its humanitarianism, and as already noted, benefits from the "goodwill Turkey has built up over its actions in the Kosovo crisis." When an invasion was being planned, NATO officials expressed hope that Turkey might send ground troops to Kosovo, where they could put their current experience to good use.[36]

Turkish assistance was also important in Bosnia, Randal reports, when Washington decided that Turkey "could be decked out as a friendly, pro-Western, moderate Muslim NATO partner" to take over training missions that the Clinton Administration regarded as "politically risky" because they would require keeping U.S. troops in Bosnia long after the Dayton accords. "In public no one mentioned the ironies of Turkey, a state involved in crushing the identity of its Kurdish minority, helping Bosnia's beleaguered Muslims to survive against proponents of 'greater' Croatia and Serbia."

Washington claims to be unable to investigate atrocities in Southeast Turkey because of Turkish bans on travel to the region. "The U.S. government's professed inability to seriously evaluate the actions of a major NATO ally does not appear credible, given the immense investigative resources at its disposal," Human Rights Watch comments, with some understatement. Furthermore, "throughout Turkey's wide-ranging scorched earth campaign, U.S. troops, aircraft and intelligence personnel have remained at their posts throughout Turkey, mingling with Turkish counterinsurgency troops and aircrews in southeastern bases such as Incirlik and Dyarbakir"—bases from which the U.S. launches regular attacks against Iraq, while Turkey invades Northern Iraq at will to punish Kurds, following the practices of its close Israeli ally, which now uses bases in Eastern Turkey for training flights for its advanced (U.S.) aircraft and for upgrading Turkish military facilities. Nuclear weapons are also deployed at these major U.S. bases, and Israel has at least the capability to do the same. While U.S. jets based at Incirlik patrol Northern Iraq and bomb air-defense systems allegedly in order to protect Iraqi Kurds, "in regular sorties north of the Iraqi border, Turkey simultaneously uses U.S.-exported jets and attack helicopters—and U.S.-supplied intelligence—to target the same Kurdish population in Iraq."[37]

The State Department Human Rights Reports have been subjected to some criticism by human rights groups for downplaying the atrocities in Turkey, just as they have been from their first appearance, with particular bitterness in the 1980s, for their apologetics for state terror in client regimes. In its critique of the report for 1994, when atrocities were peaking in Turkey with increasing U.S. assistance, the Lawyers Committee observed that the report

> gives only a sketchy picture of the most egregious collective violation of human rights in Turkey during 1994, namely the Turkish Army's stepped-up campaign of destruction of Kurdish villages, accompanied by the burning of forests and the forced displacement of populations in the southeastern region of the country. Vast stretches of previously inhabited land have been turned into scorched earth and large numbers of people—over two million by many estimates—have been forced from their homes and obliged to seek refuge in the cities. The report either ignores these violations or speaks of them in euphemistic language that echoes that used in the official pronouncements of the Turkish Government.[38]

Perhaps one should expect nothing more of official agencies. And perhaps it is naive to expect the general intellectual culture, the elite media in particular, to recognize the moral truisms mentioned earlier. But there is no reason for the public to conform to those demands, and it is the obligation of anyone who takes moral truisms seriously to act to terminate the terrible crimes in which we are engaged—without awareness, thanks to the major information systems.

NATO has "done nothing to set up oversight mechanisms to restrain Turkey's armed forces," which are often integrated into the NATO command structure, Human Rights Watch continues. While most other arms suppliers have at least made mild gestures of protest (temporary arms bans, etc.), Washington is following "our values" as understood by the political leadership, which remains silent or supportive.

As in other cases, charges of a "double standard" are quite wrong: "our values" are implemented with no slight consistency.

Turkey has been highly appreciative of the U.S. stand, Tirman reports. "We have nothing to complain about with the Clinton

Administration," one high official commented: "In northern Iraq, on NATO, Bosnia, economics and trade—it's all been very good and helpful. [Assistant Secretary of State Richard] Holbrooke and [Ambassador Marc] Grossman are excellent." A diplomat in the U.S. Embassy praised U.S. military aid to Turkey as "incentives" that help them become "a country that supports our kind of values," rather like Suharto in Indonesia—"our kind of guy," the Clinton Administration explained, before he made his first mistakes (losing control, and unwillingness to impose harsh IMF conditions on the general population). "It's not fair for us to urge Turkey to not only be a democratic country but to recognize human rights and then not to help the government of Turkey deal with terrorism right within its own borders," Vice President Al Gore added, justifying the huge flow of arms for internal repression and ethnic cleansing.[39]

Tirman notes that Turkey's war against the Kurds "raged on unknown to most Americans," who were paying for it. Others have also observed that "the brutal scorched earth campaign…, deforestation and village burnings have been accomplished with little press attention, a minimum of public debate, and no censure from the United Nations" (McKiernan). Standard practice, of obvious utility.

Turkey's treatment of its Kurdish population has not passed completely without notice, though the unpleasant facts have not been permitted to sully the admiration for the New Humanism. The issue arose in connection with the trial (if the word can be used) of Ocalan after he was kidnapped by Turkish forces in Kenya, surely with U.S. complicity.[40] New York Times correspondent Stephen Kinzer wrote that most of Turkey's 10 million Kurds have "roots in the southeastern provinces that have been shaken by violence for the last fifteen years. Some say they have been oppressed under Turkish rule, but the Government insists that they are granted the same rights as other citizens." "There have long been complaints from Kurds, a distinct ethnic group in Turkey and neighboring countries, about official suppression of their language and culture. The Kurdish guerrillas have been at war with the Turkish government for fifteen years, a struggle that according to various estimates

has taken more than 30,000 lives and cost Ankara $100 billion."
Kinzer's reports on Ocalan's capture a few months earlier, which
included marginal references to some of the facts, focused on his
rise as "one of the greatest modern tragedies for the hapless Kurds,"
apparently comparable to the "white genocide" of the Clinton years
or the gassing of Kurds by Saddam Hussein.[41]

These reports are not literally incorrect. Nor would it be literally
incorrect if the reporting on Kosovo satisfied itself with the observation that most of Serbia's Albanian minority have "roots in
Kosovo, which has been shaken by violence for the last eight years.
Some say they have been oppressed under Serbian rule, but the
Government insists that they are granted the same rights as other
citizens. There have long been complaints from Albanians, a distinct ethnic group in the FRY and some neighboring countries,
about official suppression of their language and culture. The
Albanian guerrillas have been at war with the government of
Serbia for eight years, a struggle that according to various estimates
has taken more than X lives and cost Belgrade Y dollars" (fill in X
and Y, depending on date chosen). True as far as it goes, but not
quite the whole story. The comparison, however, is not exact. U.S.-
backed repression and atrocities have been far more severe over a
long period, and their escalation to the gruesome heights of the
mid-1990s was not attributable in any way to bombardment and
threat of imminent invasion by the world's leading military power.

As noted earlier, along with reports on the Kosovo Peace
Accord, the *Times* noted that "Turkey's best-known human rights
advocate [Akin Birdal] entered prison" to serve his sentence for
having "urged the state to reach a peaceful settlement with Kurdish
rebels"—as proposed by the PKK seven years earlier, an offer rejected by Ankara and Washington in favor of ethnic cleansing, state
terror, and torture on a grand scale. Below the threshold was the
fact that as Birdal began to serve his sentence, the Turkish parliament "overwhelmingly approved a new government that has
pledged to crush Kurdish guerrillas fighting for a homeland in
southeastern Turkey." The new government promised to "wipe out
the Kurdish rebels and has ruled out negotiations with Kurdish
guerrilla leader Abdullah Ocalan, despite his repeated peace over-

tures" during his trial—in fact, since 1992. The new government thus failed to fulfill the "hopes of friends of Turkey" expressed by the national press. The day before the new government was approved, prosecutors had asked the Court "to sentence Ocalan to death for leading the Kurdistan Workers Party in its fifteen-year war for autonomy in southeast Turkey," an act that would very likely undercut what hopes remain for peaceful settlement and set the stage for further tragedy.[42]

Journals of opinion have also largely avoided the matter, particularly during the period of outrage over the Serbian demon whose actions are "wholly comparable with Hitler's and Stalin's forced deportations of entire ethnic groups" (Timothy Garton Ash in the *New York Review*, one of many such comparisons).[43] Like other commentators who try to be serious, Garton Ash recognizes that Serbia's reenactment of the days of Hitler and Stalin "escalated dramatically as soon as the air campaign began." Could that have been anticipated? Reflecting on the question, he concludes that the consequences might have been obvious to "politicians from former Yugoslavia" and other uncivilized places, but it "was not obvious to us who live in a more normal world." Our "more normal world" still does not comprehend that evil roams the earth, though since March 1999 we have "learned or been reminded of some deeply sobering lessons [about] the human capacity for evil," and even "about the United States," which radically violated the values it upholds by keeping to a "no-loss war" in Kosovo.

Borrowing Orwell's apt phrase, it "wouldn't do to mention" that the "normal world" not only cheerfully tolerates huge atrocities, but actively initiates and conducts them, lends them decisive support, and applauds them, sometimes euphorically,[44] from Southeast and Western Asia to Central America to Turkey and beyond, not to speak of an earlier history. Such annoyances do not tarnish the image of the normal world with its "saintly glow," though even in this "noble phase" we must recognize our flaws: insisting on a "no-loss war" in Kosovo, the one crime that penetrates the veil of intentional ignorance.

One has to admire the achievement. We return to other contemporary samples of the genre, which of course has a long and edifying history, not only in Anglo-American culture.

The *New York Review* was, however, unusual—perhaps unique—in interrupting the flood of heartfelt denunciations of Serbia's emulation of Hitler and Stalin with an article entitled "Justice and the Kurds," reviewing a book praised as "the most serious and convincing study of Turkey's Kurdish question to date."[45] Whatever the merits of the study reviewed, the accolade cannot be correct, if only because the study pointedly and explicitly avoids the topic of "Justice and the Kurds." As stressed in its opening sentences, the study is devoted to an entirely different topic: policy issues that face "Turkish policymakers and Turkish society, as well as Turkey's friends and allies." It is "a policy study" concerned with "the future stability and well-being of Turkey as a key American ally" and the government's "ability to deal satisfactorily with the debilitating Turkish problem." The authors begin by emphasizing that their study will not deal with "human rights in Turkey," which they mention only in scattered phrases. The Human Rights Watch reports are cited in a comment in a footnote, observing that we cannot say that "the army is blameless when it comes to human rights abuses." Government policies in the Southeast receive a few sentences of mostly tactical criticism. The review itself touches on Turkey's policies towards the Kurds in a "praising with faint damns" style that is in stark contrast to the stream of indignation about today's official enemy.

Throughout the print literature, and I presume on radio and TV as well, the imbalance of coverage and concern is remarkable, even if we put aside the moral truisms that would dictate the opposite tilt. As has been documented to the level of boredom, the pattern is consistent, to a degree that is truly impressive in free societies where the penalties for adhering to moral truisms are slight.

The U.S.-Turkey example again illustrates option (I): act to escalate the atrocities—in this case on a massive scale, and with full confidence that no troubling questions will be raised as the enlightened states proceed to escalate atrocities in the Balkans from Colombia-level to perhaps even NATO-level. Though the atrocities fall well within the designated time-frame, and indeed continue right now, they do not bear on the principles of the New Humanism, which hold that "when ethnic conflict turns into ethnic cleansing where we can make a difference, we must try." That is "clearly the case in Kosovo," so Clinton announced as he ordered the bombing, but it is clearly *not* the case within NATO itself, where even more brutal ethnic cleansing must be expedited.

U.S./U.K. contempt for Kurdish rights has a long and distinguished history, including in recent years the notorious sell-out of the Kurds to Iraqi terror in 1975 (eliciting Kissinger's observation that "covert action should not be confused with missionary work") and again in 1988, when the U.S./U.K. reacted to Saddam's gassing of Kurds by increasing their military and other support for their friend and ally; U.S. food supplies were particularly vital, not only as a taxpayer gift to U.S. agribusiness but also because Saddam's terror operations had destroyed much of Iraq's food production.[46]

In Britain's case, the record goes back far beyond. One enlightening moment was after World War I when Britain was no longer able to control its empire by ground forces and turned to the new weapons of air power and poison gas, the latter a particular favorite of Winston Churchill for use against "uncivilised tribes" and "recalcitrant Arabs" (Kurds and Afghans). It was presumably these disorderly elements that the eminent statesman Lloyd George had in mind when he applauded Britain's success in blocking an international treaty that sought to ban bombardment of civilians, having "insisted on reserving the right to bomb niggers."

Though these are understood to be among the facts "it wouldn't do to mention," one cannot be too careful; there always is the random deviant. Accordingly, William Waldegrave, who was in charge of Prime Minister John Major's "open government" initiative, ordered the removal from the Public Record Office of "files detailing how British troops had used poison gas against Iraqi dissidents (including Kurds) in 1919." This "childish sanitizing of historical embarrassments" followed the model of the statist reactionaries of the Reagan Administration, whose dedication to protecting state power from public scrutiny reached such extremes that the State Department historians resigned in public protest.[47]

Let us turn to one last illustration of the New Humanism in practice, still keeping within the designated time frame (the 1990s), a case that happens to have direct implications for the Balkans as well.

Every year thousands of people—mostly children, the rest mostly poor farmers—are killed in the Plain of Jars in Northern Laos, the scene of the heaviest bombing of civilian targets in history it appears, and arguably the most cruel: Washington's furious assault on a poor peasant society had little to do with its wars in the region. The worst period was from 1968, when Washington was compelled to agree to a negotiated settlement (under popular and business pressure) and therefore to call a halt to the regular bombardment of North Vietnam, which had turned much of it into a wasteland. With those targets lost, the planes were shifted to bombardment of Laos and Cambodia, with consequences that should be well known.

The current deaths are from "bombies," tiny anti-personnel weapons, far worse than land-mines: they are designed specifically to kill and maim, not to damage trucks or buildings. "Bombies" are the live munitions that are packed together in cluster bombs, less than the size of a clenched fist.[48] The Plain was saturated with hundreds of millions of these criminal devices, which have a failure-to-explode rate of 20%–30% according to the manufacturer, Honeywell (now a spin-off, Alliant Techsystems). The numbers suggest either remarkably poor quality control or a rational policy of murdering civilians by delayed action. These constituted only a fraction of the technology deployed, including advanced missiles to penetrate caves where families sought shelter, killing hundreds with a single missile. Current annual casualties from "bombies" are estimated from hundreds a year to "an annual nationwide casualty rate of 20,000," more than half of them deaths, according to the veteran Asia correspondent Barry Wain of the *Wall Street Journal*—in its Asia edition.[49]

A conservative estimate, then, is that the crisis each year is comparable to the toll in Kosovo in the year before the NATO bombing, though as in Colombia this is an annual toll, and deaths are far more highly concentrated among children—over half, according to studies reported by the Mennonite Central Committee, which has been working in Northern Laos since 1977 to alleviate the continuing atrocities.

There have been efforts to publicize and deal with the humanitarian catastrophe. The British-based Mine Advisory Group (MAG) has been trying to remove the lethal objects, but the U.S. is "conspicuously missing from the handful of Western organisations that have followed MAG," the British press reports, though it has finally agreed to train some Laotian civilians. The British press also reports, with some annoyance, the allegation of MAG specialists that the U.S. refuses to provide them with "render harmless procedures" that would make their work "a lot quicker and a lot safer." These remain a state secret, as does the whole affair in the United States. The Bangkok press reports a similar situation in Cambodia, particularly the Eastern region where U.S. bombardment from early 1969 was most intense.[50]

A rare mention in the U.S. press, headlined "US Clears Laos of the Unexploded," reports with pride that "crew-cut American officers are training Laotians as part of an international program to clear hundreds, if not thousands, of unexploded ordnance that pose a threat to Laotian farmers." Even apart from a few omissions, reality is a little different: MAG found 700 "bombies" in a third of a hectare in one schoolyard, and as noted, children are the main victims. The same national daily does have a front-page report headlined "One Man's Crusade to Destroy Mines," honoring a Japanese entrepreneur whose company is designing technology to clear land mines used by the Russian invaders of Afghanistan.[51]

In the case of Laos, as in East Timor, Washington's current choice of options is (II): do nothing. The failure is arguably even more evil than in the case of East Timor, given the nature of the U.S. role. And the reaction of the media and commentators is to keep silent, following the norms under which the war against Laos was designated a "secret war"—meaning well-known, but suppressed, as was the bombing of Cambodia from March 1969. The level of self-censorship was extraordinary then, as is the current phase. The events, and the reactions then and until today, tell us a good deal about the New Humanism, and about the "normal world" in which we comfortably find our home.

By April 1999, U.S. correspondents on the scene reported that NATO was using cluster bombs in Kosovo, turning "parts of the province into a no man's land," "littered" with unexploded bomblets; as noted, they were also used to kill Serb soldiers en masse when they were drawn into the open by cross-border attacks. As in Laos and elsewhere, these weapons are causing "horrific wounds," with hundreds treated in Pristina's hospital alone, about half civilians, including Albanian children killed and wounded, mostly victims of time-activated cluster bombs designed to kill and maim without warning.[52] Noting credible reports that cluster bombs are being used, the U.K. Campaign for a Transparent & Accountable Arms Trade initiated a campaign charging Tony Blair, Robin Cook, and Defense Minister George Robertson with "criminal negligence" for deployment and use of these terror weapons, and with explicit violation of the Ottawa "Convention on the prohibition of the use, stockpiling, production and transfer of anti-personnel mines and on their destruction," as well as of British legislation that brings British law into compliance with the international convention. The U.S. cannot be charged because it refused to sign the Ottawa Convention, its normal stance with regard to human rights conventions and international law generally.[53]

The Kosovo Peace Accords require that Serb forces clear minefields; apart from limited border patrol, they are permitted to enter Kosovo only for that purpose. It is entirely appropriate that they be required to remove the mines they laid in preparation for a NATO invasion, which doubtless create serious hazards for civilians. "Serb forces were responsible for mine laying, so they will be responsible for mine removal," NATO military spokesman Colonel Conrad Freytag righteously declared.[54]

As for the idea that the U.S. might have some responsibility to clear the murderous debris of its vastly more scandalous crimes, even to provide information that would allow others to do so without being subject to the fate of the thousands who are killed every year right now—evidently that is too outlandish to consider, to judge by the (null) reaction.

President Clinton explained to the nation that "there are times when looking away simply is not an option"; "we can't respond to every tragedy in every corner of the world," but that doesn't mean that "we should do nothing for no one."[55]

Clinton's point has merit. Even the most angelic person could not attend to every problem in the world, and even a saintly state (were such an entity as a "moral state" imaginable) would have to pick and choose. But the President, and numerous commentators who repeat the point, fail to add that the "times" are well-defined. The principle applies to "humanitarian crises" in the technical sense: when the interests of the powerful are endangered. Accordingly, the examples reviewed do not qualify as "humanitarian crises," so "looking away" and "not responding" are definitely options, if not obligatory. On similar grounds, Clinton's policies on Africa are legitimate: the policies, as understood by Western diplomats, of "leaving Africa to solve its own crises." For example, in the Republic of Congo, scene of a major war and huge atrocities. Here Clinton refused a U.N. request for a trivial sum for a battalion of peacekeepers; according to the U.N.'s senior Africa envoy, the respected diplomat Mohamed Sahnoun, the refusal "torpedoed" the U.N. proposal. In the case of Sierra Leone, "Washington dragged out discussions on a British proposal to deploy peacekeepers" in 1997, paving the way for another major disaster, but also of the kind for which "looking away" is the preferred option. In other cases too, "the United States has actively thwarted efforts by the United Nations to take on peacekeeping operations that might have prevented some of Africa's wars, according to European and UN diplomats," correspondent Colum Lynch reported as the plans to bomb Serbia were reaching their final stages.[56]

The common refrain that "we can't respond to every tragedy in every corner of the world" is a cowardly evasion. The same holds for the routine reaction to the occasional impolite mention that Milosevic's crimes in Kosovo are not the only ones in the contemporary world: even if we are "ignoring comparable brutalities in Africa and Asia," nonetheless we are for once doing the right thing by using force in response "to the plight of the Kosovars," and should be applauded for that.[57] Putting aside the fact that the plight was admittedly the result of the response in overwhelming measure, it is not at all true that the enlightened states are simply "ignoring comparable brutalities": rather, they commonly intervene to escalate them, or to initiate and conduct them, dramatically so within the time frame we are permitted to inspect (the 1990s), and right within NATO, to select only the current example that requires the most effort to ignore.

I will skip other examples of options (I) and (II), which abound, and also contemporary atrocities of a different scale, such as the slaughter of Iraqi civilians by means of a vicious form of biological warfare—exactly what it means to destroy water and sewage systems and electrical and other infrastructure, and to prevent repair or even supply of medicines. The New Humanists have not ignored the moral issues that arise. It was "a very hard choice," Madeleine Albright commented on national TV in 1996 when asked for her reaction to the killing of half a million Iraqi children in five years, "but the price—we think the price is worth it." And three years later, the moral calculus is unchanged while the toll of civilians mounts, and we dedicate ourselves once again with renewed passion to "the notion, defended by Secretary of State Madeleine K. Albright, that the defense of human rights is a form of mission."[58]

Current estimates remain about 4000 children killed a month. The embargo—primarily a U.S./U.K. affair—has strengthened Saddam Hussein while devastating the civilian society. According to the respected U.N. diplomat Denis Halliday, who probably knows Iraq better than any Westerner and publicly resigned as humanitarian coordinator in Baghdad in protest over policies that he saw as "genocidal," there are costs beyond the enormous toll of death, disease, and social disintegration: "Iraq's younger generation of professionals, the political leadership of the future—bitter, angry, isolated, and dangerously alienated from the world—is maturing in an environment not dissimilar to that found in Germany under the conditions set by the Versailles Treaty," and many of them "find the present leadership and its continuing dialogue and compromise with the UN to be unacceptable, to be too 'moderate'." He warns of a "longer-term social and political impact of sanctions together with today's death and despair."[59]

Two hawkish military analysts observe that "economic sanctions may well have been a necessary [sic] cause of the deaths of more people in Iraq than have been slain by all so-called weapons of mass destruction throughout history." Reporting from Baghdad, David Shorrock reviews the effects of "the monstrous social experiment on the people of Iraq" that the West is conducting, suggesting that it is a likely model for Serbia, not implausibly.[60]

Departing from "intentional ignorance," we may recall that this is the standard operating procedure of the enlightened states when someone steps out of line as Saddam Hussein did in August 1990, shifting quickly from favored friend to demon when he committed crimes that were bad enough, but neither novel (the primary fear of the Bush Administration was that unless negotiations were blocked he would duplicate what the U.S. had just accomplished in Panama), nor very grave by his gruesome standards, which posed no serious problem for the enlightened states. Or Nicaragua, no problem while Somoza's U.S.-supplied and -trained army was killing tens of thousands of people twenty years ago, but reduced to the second poorest country in the hemisphere (after Haiti) for the crime of disobedience shortly after. Or Cuba, subjected to forty years of terror and unprecedented economic warfare, with sanctions that bar even food and (effectively) medicine, not because of Castro's crimes, but, so we learn from the Kennedy intellectuals, out of concern over "the spread of the Castro idea of taking matters into one's own hands," a serious problem because throughout Latin America "the distribution of land and other forms of national wealth greatly favors the propertied classes, [and] the poor and underprivileged, stimulated by the example of the Cuban revolution, are now demanding opportunities for a decent living."[61]

These and many other examples might be kept in mind when we read admiring accounts of how the "moral compass" of the Clinton Administration is at last functioning properly—in Kosovo.[62]

It might be argued that this sample is unfair, omitting the cases put forth as the prize examples of the New Humanism: Somalia and

Haiti. The challenge has some merit, but also a defect: the merest look at these cases makes the story only more sordid.

Uncontroversially, Washington played a major role in creating the tragedy of the early '90s in Somalia, then stood aside until the fighting had declined and relief was beginning to flow freely. That its December 1992 intervention was a public relations stunt was recognized even in the usually supportive media, which ridiculed "the invasion's made-for-Hollywood quality," describing it as a "showcase" for the military budget, "a public relations bonanza at just the right time." It was a "paid political advertisement" on behalf of plans for an intervention force, Joint Chiefs Chair Colin Powell commented. But things soon went sour, in large part because of U.S. military doctrine, which calls for massive force if U.S. soldiers come under any threat.[63]

In October 1993, "criminal incompetence by the US military led to the slaughter of more than 1,000 Somalis by American fire-power," the press later reported. The official estimate was 6–10,000 Somali casualties in the summer of 1993 alone, two-thirds women and children. Estimates are highly uncertain. "Somali casualties have been largely overlooked by reporters," the occasional reference noted.[64]

The last U.S. Marines left Somalia behind a hail of gunfire—a ratio of about 100 to one, *Los Angeles Times* correspondent John Balzar reported. The U.S. command did not count Somali casualties, Balzar reports, surely not those killed because they "just appeared to be threatening." Marine Lt. Gen. Anthony Zinni, who commanded the operation, informed the press that "I'm not counting bodies...I'm not interested." "CIA officials privately concede that the U.S. military may have killed from 7,000 to 10,000 Somalis" while losing thiry-four soldiers, the editor of *Foreign Policy*, Charles William Maynes, noted in passing. After Zinni led the December 1998 bombing of Iraq, a *New York Times* profile took note of his immersion in foreign cultures and history, which made him "sensitive to Arab values."[65]

The number of lives saved by the "humanitarian intervention" is estimated by the U.S. Refugee Policy Group at 10–25,000; even the lower figure may be an overestimate, Alex de Waal of African

Rights observes, since most of the deaths were caused by malaria and there were no anti-malaria programs; de Waal is a leading specialist on famine, aid, and this region specifically. Specific war crimes of U.S. forces included direct military attacks on a hospital and on civilian gatherings. Other Western armies were implicated in serious crimes as well. Some of these were revealed at an official Canadian inquiry, not duplicated by the U.S. or other governments.[66]

The usual picture is as portrayed by the *Washington Post*, opening the new year: U.S. troops were "leading the way" in a U.N. operation, but "the thousands of Somali lives saved were overshadowed by the deaths of eighteen U.S. soldiers," a disaster that led to "U.N. withdrawal." The thousands of Somali lives lost have rarely appeared on the radar screen, and are unmentioned.[67]

In Haiti, the first free election took place in December 1989 in a ruined country that the U.S. had dominated since Woodrow Wilson's murderous invasion.[68] To general surprise, the winning candidate, with a two-thirds majority, was the populist priest Jean-Bertrand Aristide, backed by a vigorous grass-roots movement that had escaped notice. Appalled by the defeat of its own candidate, who received 14% of the vote, Washington moved at once to undermine Haiti's first democratic government. When it was overthrown seven months later by a murderous military regime, Washington maintained close intelligence and military ties with the new rulers while undermining the embargo called by the Organization of American States, even authorizing illegal shipments of oil to the regime and its wealthy supporters.

After three years of terror, the U.S. intervened to "restore democracy," but on condition that the Aristide government adopt the U.S. program that had been decisively rejected in the sole free election. Washington imposed an extremely harsh version of these neoliberal policies. One consequence was destruction of rice production, the food staple in which Haiti had been self-sufficient. Under the U.S.-imposed reforms, Haitian farmers were denied tariff protection and were therefore free to compete with U.S. agribusiness, which receives 40% of its profits from government subsidies, sharply increased under Reagan. Recognizing what was in store, a 1995 USAID report observed that the "export-driven trade and investment policy" that Washington mandates will "relentlessly squeeze the domestic rice farmer," who will be forced to turn to agroexport in accord with the principles of rational expectations theory, and with incidental benefit to U.S. agribusiness and investors. More recently, one of the few hopeful enterprises in the stricken country, production of chicken parts, was destroyed in the same fashion. U.S. producers have a large surplus of dark meat that is "flooding Haiti," compelled to reduce tariff protection to near-zero by the U.S.-mandated neoliberal program, unlike Canada and Mexico, which impose tariffs of over 200% to bar U.S. dumping.[69]

In principle Haiti could resort to anti-dumping measures, closing its markets to U.S. exporters in retaliation, following Washington's regular practice to protect domestic producers. The double-edged market theory that has reigned for hundreds of years—market discipline for you, but the nanny state for me—is revealed in stark ugliness when practiced by the world's richest country to destroy a brutalized corner of the world that may well become uninhabitable before too long.

U.S. troops seized 160,000 pages of documents of the coup regime and its paramilitary forces, still kept from Haiti's government apart from redacted versions with names of U.S. citizens removed—"to avoid embarrassing revelations" about U.S. government involvement with the terrorist regime and efforts to undermine programs undertaken during the brief democratic interlude, according to Human Rights Watch and analysts cited by the Council on Hemispheric Affairs. The Clinton Administration withdrew U.S. forces in 1996 after Deputy Secretary of State Strobe Talbott, now prominent in the Balkans, assured Congress that "we will remain in charge by means of USAID and the private sector."[70]

We may also recall, perhaps, that Haiti was one of the richest colonies of the world and a source of a good part of France's wealth, ranked alongside of Bengal, now Bangladesh—observations that might provoke some thoughts if we can escape the grip of "intentional ignorance." It is revealing enough to observe, however, that Haiti is the prize example offered to demonstrate Washington's sincere dedication to human rights, in this case the virtues of "humanitarian intervention."

Haiti also provides much insight into the operative meaning of Article 14 of the Universal Declaration of Human Rights, which guarantees the right of asylum from persecution. Twenty years ago, the Carter Administration initiated the forceful return of fleeing boat people to the mercies of the Duvalier dictatorship. The violation of Article 14 was formally ratified in a Reagan-Duvalier agreement. During the brief and despised democratic interlude, when terror virtually ceased and the refugee flow reduced to a trickle, policy was reversed and Article 14 honored. When the military coup renewed the terror, Washington returned to its "reprehensible, ...illegal and irresponsible refugee policy" (Americas Watch). The policy was bitterly condemned by candidate Bill Clinton, whose first act as President was to make it harsher still. The Supreme Court endorsed the forceful return of Haitian refugees, apparently relying for its interpretation of international refugee law on Switzerland's arguments for barring Jews fleeing the Holocaust, the Editor in Chief of the *American Journal of International Law* commented in a 1998 review of the "alarming exacerbation" of Washington's refusal to adhere to treaty obligations in the past ten years, even beyond Reaganite radicalism, which broke new grounds in this and other respects.[71]

In short, the prize examples do not lend powerful support to the imagery of the New Humanism, though they do shed light on the values that guide it.

3.3 "Humanitarian Intervention."

Let us now turn to the third choice of policy in the case of humanitarian crises, option (III): try to mitigate the catastrophe. This could take take the form of peaceful means (diplomacy, constructive aid), or it could involve the use of force: what is called "humanitarian intervention."

To find examples illustrating humanitarian intervention is all too easy, at least if we keep to official rhetoric. In this realm, it is close to a universal truth that the use of force is driven by humanitarian commitments. The world beyond looks a bit different.

The issue naturally arose as soon as the NATO bombings commenced. There is a regime of international law and international order, largely crafted by the United States, and binding on all states. Its fundamentals are articulated in the United Nations Charter, then subsequent General Assembly Resolutions and World Court decisions. In brief, the threat or use of force is banned unless explicitly authorized by the Security Council after it has determined that peaceful means have failed, or in self-defense against "armed attack" (a narrow concept) until the Security Council acts (Article 51).

There is, of course, more to say. Thus there is at least a tension, if not an outright contradiction, between the rules of world order laid down in the Charter and the rights articulated in the UD, a second pillar of the world order established under U.S. initiative after World War II. The Charter bans force violating state sovereignty; the UD guarantees the rights of individuals against oppressive states, though neither the UD nor the enabling resolutions indicate any enforcement mechanism. The issue of humanitarian intervention arises from this tension. It is the right of humanitarian intervention that was claimed by the U.S./NATO in Kosovo, with the general support of media and a broad range of commentary.

The question was addressed at once in a *New York Times* report headed: "Legal Scholars Support Case for Using Force."[72] One example is offered: Allen Gerson, former counsel to the U.S. mission to the U.N. Two other legal scholars are cited. One, Ted Galen Carpenter, "scoffed at the Administration argument" and dismissed the alleged right of intervention. The third is Jack Goldsmith, a specialist on international law at Chicago Law School. He says that critics of the NATO bombing "have a pretty good legal argument," but "many people think [an exception for humanitarian intervention] does exist as a matter of custom and practice." That summarizes the evidence offered to justify the favored conclusion stated in the headline. The matter was largely dropped thereafter, the assertion in the headline having been proven by this evidence.

Goldsmith's observation is reasonable, at least if we agree that facts are relevant to the determination of "custom and practice."

We may also bear in mind another truism: the right of humanitarian intervention, if it exists, is premised on the good faith of those
intervening, and that assumption is based not on their rhetoric but
on their record. That is indeed a truism, at least with regard to others. Consider, for example, Iranian offers to intervene in Bosnia to
prevent massacres at a time when the West would not do so. These
were dismissed with ridicule (in fact, generally ignored), even
though they might well have protected Muslims from slaughter at
Srebrenica and elsewhere. If there was a reason beyond subordination to power, it was because Iranian good faith could not be
assumed—reasonably enough; thus Iran is one of the two countries
to have rejected a World Court judgment, along with other criminal acts. A rational person then asks obvious questions: Is the
Iranian record of intervention and terror worse than that of the
United States, the second of the two countries to have rejected a
World Court judgment, along with other criminal acts?[73] And other
questions: For example, how should we assess the good faith of the
only country to have vetoed a Security Council resolution calling
on all states to obey international law? What about its historical
record? Unless such questions are prominent, an honest person will
dismiss the discourse as worthless subordination to doctrine.

It is a useful exercise to determine how much of the literature—
media or other—survives such elementary considerations as these.

The most extensive recent academic study of "humanitarian
intervention" is by George Washington University Law Professor
Sean Murphy, formerly Counselor for Legal Affairs at the U.S.
Embassy in the Hague. He reviews the record after the Kellogg-
Briand pact of 1928 which outlawed war, and then after the U.N.
Charter, which strengthened and articulated these provisions. In
the first phase, he writes, the most prominent examples of "humanitarian intervention" were Japan's attack on Manchuria, Mussolini's
invasion of Ethiopia, and Hitler's occupation of parts of
Czechoslovakia, all accompanied by uplifting humanitarian
rhetoric and factual justifications. Japan was going to establish an
"earthly paradise" as it defended Manchurians from "Chinese ban-
dits," with the support of a leading Chinese nationalist, a more
credible figure than anyone the U.S. was able to conjure up during

its attack on South Vietnam. Mussolini was liberating thousands of slaves as he carried forth the Western civilizing mission. Hitler announced Germany's intention to end ethnic tensions and violence, and "safeguard the national individuality of the German and Czech peoples" in an operation "filled with earnest desire to serve the true interests of the peoples dwelling in the area," in accordance with their will. In further legitimation, the Slovakian President asked Hitler to declare Slovakia a protectorate.[74]

Another useful intellectual exercise is to compare those obscene justifications with those offered for interventions, including "humanitarian interventions," in the U.N. Charter era.

In that period, perhaps the most compelling example of option (III) is the Vietnamese invasion of Cambodia in December 1978, terminating Pol Pot's atrocities, which were then peaking. Vietnam pleaded the right of self-defense against armed attack, one of the few Charter-era examples when the plea is plausible: the Khmer Rouge regime (Democratic Kampuchea, DK) was carrying out murderous attacks against Vietnam in border areas. The U.S. reaction is instructive. The press condemned the "Prussians" of Asia for their outrageous violation of international law. They were harshly punished for the crime of having ended Pol Pot's slaughters, first by a (U.S.-backed) Chinese invasion, then by U.S. imposition of extremely harsh sanctions. Washington recognized the expelled DK as the official government of Cambodia, because of its "continuity" with the Pol Pot regime, the State Department explained. Not too subtly, it proceeded to support the Khmer Rouge in its continuing attacks in Cambodia.

The example tells us more about the "custom and practice" that underlies the actual "emerging legal norms of humanitarian intervention."

Another illustration of (III) is India's invasion of East Pakistan in 1971, which terminated an enormous massacre and refugee flight (over ten million, according to estimates at the time). The U.S. condemned India for aggression, threatening war. Kissinger was particularly infuriated by India's action, in large part, it seems, because it was interfering with a carefully staged secret trip to China from Pakistan, which was going to provide wonderful photo-ops.[75]

Perhaps this is one of the examples that historian John Lewis Gaddis had in mind in his admiring review of the latest volume of Kissinger's memoirs, when he reports that Kissinger "acknowledges here, more clearly than in the past, the influence of his upbringing in Nazi Germany, the examples set by his parents and the consequent impossibility, for him, of operating outside a moral framework."[76] The logic is overpowering, as are the illustrations, too well-known to record.

Again, the same lessons.

The record of "humanitarian intervention" does not, of course, begin with the Kellogg-Briand Pact in 1928. It has a distinguished ancestry. As noted, it may be close to a universal feature of aggression and violence. To be sure, there are exceptions. The ones most familiar to us are those that lie at the core of our moral and ethical tradition, deriving from the divine commandments to perpetrate genocide recorded in the Bible, executed faithfully by the chosen people and emulated by their successors, among them the Frankish knights who ravaged the Levant a millennium ago with the same divine dispensation and the "children of Israel" who followed God's will in the New World, among numerous episodes of the "sacralization of war."

If we had records we might find that Genghis Khan and Attila the Hun professed humanitarian motives. U.S. history alone offers many illustrations, for example, Theodore Roosevelt's explanation of the humanitarian motives of the conquest of the West, virtually eliminating its indigenous population (a result already achieved in the East): "the most ultimately righteous of all wars is a war with savages," establishing the rule of "the dominant world races."[77]

As the conquerors completed their "most ultimately righteous" wars—"the task of felling trees and Indians and of rounding out their natural boundaries" as it is described in a leading modern diplomatic history[78]—they moved beyond, always inspired by elevated humanitarian motives. They managed to intervene in Cuba in 1898 just in time to prevent its liberation from Spain, turning it into a "virtual colony" of the United States (in the words of two Harvard historians), thus fulfilling the earliest foreign policy goal of the newly-liberated United States.[79] The intervention was self-lauded as "in the interest of civilization, humanity, and liberty." "We took up arms only in obedience to the dictates of humanity and in fulfillment of high public and moral obligations," President McKinley orated, acting "in the name of humanity," "in the name of civilization." Theodore Roosevelt and Woodrow Wilson emphatically agreed, along with leading intellectuals and scholars until the present.

It took a bit more effort to portray the conquest of the Philippines in the same light, as old Indian fighters left hundreds of thousands of corpses in their wake in another one of the "the most ultimately righteous of all wars." But that too was accomplished, to general acclaim that persists to the present.[80] The President recognized that he had not quite obtained the consent of the Filipinos "to perform a great act for humanity," as he was doing. But there was no need:

> We were obeying a higher moral obligation, which rested on us and which did not require anybody's consent. We were doing our duty by them, as God gave us the light to see our duty, with the consent of our own consciences and with the approval of civilization... It is not a good time for the liberator to submit important questions concerning liberty and government to the liberated while they are engaged in shooting down their rescuers.

The U.S. was simply extending the practices of its models and predecessors. After centuries of experience, the Concert of Europe of the late 19th century renewed the commitment of the civilized nations to relieve the plight of the backward peoples of the world, from China to Africa to the Middle East, including the Serbs— "Orientals, therefore liars, tricksters and masters of evasion," the Kaiser proclaimed from the heartland of European culture.[81] The consequences need not be reviewed.

More intelligent leaders have perceived what they were doing and sometimes described it with a degree of accuracy, for example, Winston Churchill, in a paper submitted to his Cabinet colleagues in January 1914 explaining the need for increased military expenditures:

> we are not a young people with *an innocent record and* a scanty inher-
> itance. We have engrossed to ourselves...*an altogether disproportionate*
> share of the wealth and traffic of the world. We have got all we want
> in territory, and our claim to be left in the unmolested enjoyment of
> vast and splendid possessions, *mainly acquired by violence, largely
> maintained by force*, often seems less reasonable to others than to us.

Churchill understood that these insights are not for popular con-
sumption in a free society. The italicized phrases were excised in
the version he made public in his book *The World Crisis* in the
1920s. Recently released, they are unlikely to have a more prominent place in the intellectual culture and educational system than
many others like them, for example, Churchill's enthusiastic advo-
cacy of the use of poison gas against Kurds and other uncivilized
tribes, and its implementation, now safely excised from the
records.[82]

Given the richness and familiarity of the historical record, it is
remarkable to observe the untroubled rise of the New Humanism,
even its exaltation, sometimes on the part of people with an
admirable record on human rights. Michael Glennon, for example,
who fifteen years ago deplored the device of "intentional ignorance" employed to evade the horrors that the leader of the
enlightened states was then perpetrating, no less righteously than
before or since. Adopting that stance today, Glennon presents the
venerable doctrines as a new departure justly undertaken by the
"enlightened states," who must now discard the misguided "old
anti-interventionist structure" instituted after World War II, recognizing that "the failings of the old system were so disastrous."[83]
Disastrous they no doubt were. To mention only the most glaring
illustration, such massive atrocities as the U.S. wars in Indochina
could not even be brought before the United Nations for fear that
the U.N. would be destroyed by the leading enlightened state,
hardly the only case (and one that Glennon does not mention,
though he rightly lists the Soviet invasion of Afghanistan). And we
may recall what happened when the World Court dared to offend
the master by charging it with "unlawful use of force" and ordering
it to desist and pay substantial reparations, just as we know—or
should know—which two states have blocked United Nations

action by veto ever since the organization fell out of control in the course of decolonization, over thirty years ago.

But these are not the kinds of examples that Glennon and others have in mind. Those he does give are instructive, but I will put them aside, noting only the prime example he offers of the promise of the "new interventionism": NATO's pursuit of "international justice" in Kosovo to terminate "ethnic cleansing," which "evidently is what NATO and the United States have recently set out to do." This is so "evident" that neither argument nor evidence is needed, again the standard posture, as is the account of the timing of the ethnic cleansing and the NATO actions allegedly undertaken to terminate it.

In the light of a history that is hardly obscure it is, perhaps, a little odd to read that the "enlightened states" are opening a new era in human affairs when they grant themselves the right to use military force where they "believe it to be just," even when the praise is tempered with qualifications[84]:

> The new interventionists must reconcile the need for broad acceptance of their regime with the resistance of the defiant, the indolent, and the miscreant. Proponents of the new regime must assess whether the cost of alienating the disorderly outweighs whatever benefits can be wrought in the form of a more orderly world. Ultimately, the question will be empirical; unless a critical mass of nations accepts the solution that NATO and the United States stand ready to offer, that solution will soon be resented. But the new interventionists should not be daunted by fears of destroying some lofty, imagined temple of law enshrined in the U.N. Charter's anti-interventionist proscriptions.

Lifting the veil of intentional ignorance, we discover that "the new interventionism" is simply "the old interventionism," and that there is nothing novel in the distinction between the "enlightened states" and those who resist their righteous acts: "the defiant, the indolent, and the miscreant" (who else could object to their civilizing mission?). Tradition is also maintained when the categories are established by definition, as necessary truths, evidence deemed irrelevant or perhaps a vulgar display of "inveterate anti-Americanism."[85] And we need hardly await an "ultimate empirical" test of the consequences of these doctrines—or, for that matter, even of the sole question that can be conceived within the framework of enlightenment, the cost-benefit calculation presented. There is a vast store of evidence bearing on the consequences of the doctrines that are now to be reinstated, as they have been implemented by the enlightened states that again assign themselves the mission they have been conducting with such estimable results for centuries.

Case books on international humanitarian law and other scholarly sources commonly recognize that genuine cases of intervention undertaken with humanitarian intent are hard to find, though humanitarian pretensions are common, and military actions taken on other grounds sometimes have benign consequences, as in several cases mentioned, or the defeat of Nazi Germany, to mention the most spectacular example. The one illustration of genuine humanitarian intervention that is regularly offered is the French intervention in the Levant in 1860. It may seem unlikely that the historical record should offer such a singular exception to the norm, and as might be expected, the example does not sustain inspection, as the scholarly literature makes quite evident.[86]

The record may well be unblemished, at least by any clear example. The category of genuine humanitarian intervention might turn out to be literally null, if investigation is unencumbered by intentional ignorance. Even if genuine examples can be unearthed, the current fascination with the topic might raise some questions, in the light of past and present history.

The topic deserves a much fuller examination. That course is not easy to undertake, for one reason, because of the "general tacit agreement that 'it wouldn't do' to mention that particular fact," including the most relevant facts, and the startling refusal of the prophets of the New Humanism to offer any argument, even the most minimal, in support of their remarkable claims, beyond the fact that they are "evidently" true. Several illustrations have been given; we return to others.

CHAPTER 4

The Denial Syndrome

A s already reviewed, the resort to bombing, whatever its intention may have been, "greatly accelerated [the] slaughter and dispossession" of the Albanian Kosovars,[1] "the result" that was anticipated, notably by the Commander of the NATO forces, who not only took these consequences to be "entirely predictable" from the start, but also informed the press that "the political leadership" never had "any intent" to block "Serb ethnic cleansing," and that the war plans they ordered him to prepare were "not designed" to have any such effect, "not in any way." Putting to the side this interesting testimony on criminal negligence, let us turn to the methods that have been employed to present the facts in a more attractive light.

The simplest method has been to declare that the facts are false, adopting the position of the President as he "responded to critics in the United States and Europe who say the removal of human-rights observers from Kosovo [on March 19] and the beginning of the air attacks [on March 24] touched off Mr. Milosevic's expulsion of non-Serbs from Kosovo." "Ethnic cleansing in Kosovo was not a response to bombing," Clinton declared, settling the matter.[2]

Proceeding, Clinton described the ethnic cleansing that followed the bombing as "the 10-year method of Mr. Milosevic's madness," so that "He could not be prevented, therefore, from driving the Albanian Kosovars from their land." Clinton's account evidently heightens his guilt in having preferred to deal with Milosevic in 1995, sacrificing the Kosovo Albanians. He states further that well before the bombing, Milosevic's actions within Kosovo had given ample notice of his intentions to expel the population, which, if true, raises Clinton's culpability to even greater heights, considering the preparations for this huge refugee flow that "could not be prevented." A lesser problem arose in his victory speech a few days later, when he informed the nation that the campaign had achieved its goal of creating the conditions to bring home the refugees—a claim that is "somewhat at variance with the fact that the purge of the Albanians became much more extensive after the bombing began on March 24," when "Mr. Clinton declared that NATO's purpose was to avert 'a humanitarian disaster'."[3]

At the outset Washington had insisted that it both knew and didn't know that a catastrophe would ensue. On March 28, "when a reporter asked if the bombing was accelerating the atrocities, [President Clinton] replied, 'absolutely not'." He reiterated that stand in an April 1 speech at Norfolk Naval Air Station: "Had we not acted, the Serbian offensive would have been carried out with impunity." The following day, Pentagon spokesman Kenneth Bacon announced that the opposite was true: "I don't think anyone could have foreseen the breadth of this brutality," the "first acknowledgment" by the Administration that "it was not fully prepared for the crisis," the press reported—a crisis that was "entirely predictable," the Commanding General had informed the press a week earlier. From the start, reports from the scene were that "the Administration had been caught off guard" by the Serbian military reaction.[4]

A variant is that the inevitability of the murderous expulsion of Albanians is proven by the meticulous advance planning, *Operation Horseshoe*; as already discussed, if taken at face value, the argument heightens further the culpability of the New Humanists.

Denial of the (elsewhere acknowledged) facts and evasion of what is implied by the attempts at exculpation must be accompanied by burial of the rest of inconvenient current history deep in the memory hole, in the manner already illustrated. We can then perform our duty, concentrating solely on Serb atrocities, asserting that the bombing was "evidently" undertaken to prevent the "slaughter and dispossession" of the Albanian Kosovars that it at once "greatly accelerated," as anticipated, and joining the editors of the *Wall Street Journal* in orating that "Obviously, the main impetus for military intervention [in Kosovo] is humanitarian."[5]

Reference to the *Journal* editors is misleading, however. For one thing, the picture is common. For another, it is more instructive to turn to the liberal side of the spectrum, for example, the *New York Times*. To select a typical day, the editors explain that we should not be hobbled by the analogy of Vietnam, where it was unclear that the national interest was at stake and "the sacrifices" to us might have been "too dear"; one can imagine no other reason to object to attacking South Vietnam, then the rest of Indochina, leaving millions dead and tens of millions of refugees and three countries devastated. The front-page think-piece by Craig Whitney explores the "irony" that intervention in Kosovo is supported by liberals, who opposed the Vietnam war—the liberals' war, which they finally came to oppose for the reasons explained by the editors the same day, essentially the reasons that led elements of the German General Staff to oppose a two-front war after Stalingrad. And to still any remaining doubts, Judith Miller cites a "senior diplomat" who traces U.S. policy to the fact that this "'idea' nation whose national identity derives more from a 'value-driven agenda'...has long been an aggressive promoter of human rights." Another "evident" truth, whatever the facts: for example, about the "value-driven agenda" pursued within the realm of the Monroe doctrine in aggressive promotion of human rights for a century, where opportunities were not lacking and the Cold War was more a pretext than a reason; or even closer to home, the fact that AI had just then opened a campaign to address the "persistent and widespread pattern of human rights violations in the USA," and that Human Rights Watch had just published a major study under the rubric *Human Rights Violations in the United States*. Every state is an "aggressive promoter of human rights" elsewhere.[6]

Given the force of Orwell's maxim, such methods are virtually guaranteed success. But it is possible to offer more cogent arguments. Perhaps the least implausible would be to claim that the

ethnic cleansing was already underway and that the bombing was
an effort—which failed miserably—to stop it. We would then have
to conclude that General Clark had forgotten these facts, that the
UNHCR data on registered refugees are wrong, and that journalists
on the scene who consistently and extensively reported that atrocities sharply escalated immediately after the bombing have been fal-
sifying the record. This heroic effort was undertaken by the State
Department in a report issued in May that deserves more attention
than it has received.[7]

The Executive Summary states that ethnic cleansing in Kosovo
"dramatically accelerated in mid-March 1999," meaning ten days
before the bombing, which could therefore be understood as a
response to this dramatic acceleration. The text, however, tells a
different story. Its chronology begins "after the departure of the
OSCE's Kosovo Verification Mission [KVM] on March 19," in
preparation for the bombing, and over the objections of Serbia, not
mentioned and yet to be reported.[8] Keeping to this time frame, the
chronology reports that from April 4 to mid-May over 300 villages
were burned and some 500 residential areas at least partially
burned. Other atrocities are also reported "since late March."

"Serbian forces have made Pristina, the capital of Kosovo, a
ghost town"—after the bombing, as extensively reported from the
scene, another fact unmentioned, though many pages later it is
reported that residents were expelled from Pristina from April 1
(elsewhere, from April 4). The fate of Pec was the same, but again
after the bombing (omitted). Other atrocities are reported "after
NATO airstrikes began." The report cites UNHCR "estimates that
over 700,000 Kosovars have fled [Kosovo] since the March 19,
1999 departure" of the OSCE monitors; in fact, since March 27,
according to UNHCR (see p. 16). Many other atrocities are reported, following the NATO bombing.

While the chronology begins on March 19, it reports "extensive
mobilization of Serbian security forces beyond earlier force deploy-
ments several days prior to the March 19 withdrawal of the KVM
monitors," "following the failure of the Paris talks and in anticipation of NATO airstrikes." That seems highly credible, even in the
absence of evidence. Furthermore, "The humanitarian situation,

which had improved somewhat in February, significantly deteriorated by mid-March." Again the conclusion is credible, particularly by virtue of its consistency with other reports, notably that of Marc Weller, well-placed as Legal Advisor to the Kosova (Albanian) Delegation at the Rambouillet Conference, who writes that after withdrawal of the KVM, "within a few days the number of displaced had again risen to over 200,000," two-thirds the level of Colombia in the same year.[9] The State Department provides data only for late March, apart from the killing of one person on March 18 and a March 20 attack on three towns "on the pretense that the KLA had attacked police stations there"—an example of the "terrorism" that the U.S. had condemned sharply a year earlier. On March 20, after the monitors were withdrawn, Serb forces "launched a significant operation against KLA forces," and on March 23 they "targeted" Pristina, Pec, and other cities "for ethnic cleansing," then carried out, after the bombing.

Assuming every word in the report to be accurate, we conclude that Milosevic is (once again) revealed to be a major war criminal. And the crimes of Clinton, Blair, and their associates are again clearly exposed.

The second major documentary source on the period is the indictment of Milosevic and his associates by the International Tribunal on war crimes in Yugoslavia in the Hague.[10] The charges are surely warranted, in fact long overdue. And they are far too narrow: limited to 1999 in Kosovo. According to court officials, NATO "opened the way for what amounted to a remarkably fast indictment by giving [prosecutor Louise] Arbour access to intelligence and other information long denied to her by Western governments." More accurately, we may surmise, the U.S. provided Ms. Arbour with such "intelligence and other information," or perhaps, as the accompanying story relates, "the Clinton Administration and the British Government provided intelligence information for use in formulating the indictments."

Thanks to these U.S./U.K. initiatives, "the court was able to overcome political resistance in Western capitals to an indictment whose timing was diplomatically devastating." In particular, "the United States had expressed serious concerns about the timing when informed a few days ago about the indictment" that it had expedited with such vigor. Ms. Arbour also assured the world that the court is an entirely independent actor, in no way influenced by what governments say and do, surely not by the United States, which both expedited the indictment and simultaneously "expressed serious concerns" that the court proceeded with it. The day before, "American officials insisted...that the United States had not pressured [the court] to delay or hasten the indictment of Mr. Milosevic," whom the Tribunal has been "investigating for years" (but without the crucial intelligence and other information suddenly provided by the U.S./U.K.).[11] The indictment "branded the Yugoslav government as a criminal regime, an extraordinary development." British officials expressed their government's hope that "the indictment might be helpful in stiffening [the] spine" of the Clinton Administration, while describing the diplomatic track being pursued by Soviet envoy Victor Chernomyrdin as "an unattractive bet."

How these various theses are to be reconciled is less than clear, but let us ignore the problems and accept that the U.S. both opposed and favored the rapid indictment, and that the court has exhibited its independence by its "remarkably fast" reaction to unprecedented U.S./U.K. actions to accelerate the indictment that the Clinton Administration opposed, the indictment that Washington hoped would not be issued when it provided information and intelligence previously withheld.

British Foreign Secretary Robin Cook reacted by reiterating a leading thesis of the New Humanism. "There can be no deal, no amnesty for war crimes," he said, perhaps with his NATO partners Turkey and the U.S. in mind, or perhaps even London. No fear of that: any criminal proceedings will be properly focused by those with the guns and dollars.

Turning to the indictment, we find that it is "based exclusively on crimes committed since the beginning of 1999." It refers to crimes "Beginning on or about January 1 1999." A long list of examples is provided, all of them after the onset of the NATO bombing on March 24. The indictment notes that "Since the air strikes commenced, forces of the F.R.Y. and Serbia have intensified their systematic campaign and have forcibly expelled hundreds of thousands of Kosovo Albanians." The exceptions are the Racak massacre of January 15, 1999, and "a declaration of imminent threat of war" on March 23 as NATO made final preparations for the bombing the next day (there is also a nonspecific reference to "late March").

In short, the indictment follows the same course as the State Department report just reviewed, seeking to foster the interpretation of the NATO bombing as a response to crimes beginning almost three months earlier, while offering evidence of crimes that followed the bombing.

Other arguments offered for the bombing are no more cogent, often completely irrational, referring to events that occurred *after* the decision to bomb.[12] The primary argument in this category is that NATO had to bomb to prevent the ethnic cleansing that was "the result" of its bombing, as anticipated; a small sample has already been given. A common accompaniment is that the refugees brutally expelled (after the bombing) are calling on NATO to destroy their torturers, a great surprise. Apart from the transparent irrationality, little has been heard calling for the bombing of Ankara, Tel Aviv, Washington, and other capitals, on similar grounds, nor has the press acclaimed the bombing of U.S. embassies or the World Trade Center, still pursuing the same logic.

A leading intellectual journal presented Vaclav Havel for "a reasoned explanation" of why the NATO bombing must be supported. "For Havel, the war in Yugoslavia is a landmark in international relations: the first time that the human rights of a people—the Kosovo Albanians—have unequivocally come first."[13]

Havel opened by stressing the great significance and import of the Kosovo intervention. It shows that we may at last be entering an era of true enlightenment that will witness "the end of the nation-state," which will no longer be "the culmination of every national community's history and its highest earthly value," as in the past. The "enlightened efforts of generations of democrats, the terrible experience of two world wars,...and the evolution of civilization have finally brought humanity to the recognition that human beings are more important than the state," so the Kosovo intervention reveals.

Havel then presents his "reasoned explanation" of why the intervention is just. It reads as follows:

> there is one thing that no reasonable person can deny: this is probably the first war that has not been waged in the name of "national interests," but rather in the name of principles and values… [NATO] is fighting out of concern for the fate of others. It is fighting because no decent person can stand by and watch the systematic state-directed murder of other people… The alliance has acted out of respect for human rights, as both conscience and legal documents dictate. This is an important precedent for the future. It has been clearly said that it is simply not permissible to murder people, to drive them from their homes, to torture them, and to confiscate their property,

though attention to the real world requires a qualification: when Washington so commands. It remains permissible, indeed obligatory, not only to tolerate such actions but to contribute massively to them, ensuring that they reach still greater peaks of fury—within NATO, for example—and of course to conduct them on one's own, when that is necessary. And it remains permissible if not obligatory to maintain a respectful silence on matters that "it wouldn't do to mention." The effects in the Balkans are also passed over without comment, a wise decision.

Havel had revealed the ethical standards that ground his insights and moral lessons ten years earlier, immediately after his fellow dissidents were brutally murdered in El Salvador, and the U.S. had invaded Panama, killing and destroying. To celebrate these grand events, Havel flew to Washington to address a joint session of Congress where he received a thunderous standing ovation for lauding the "defender of freedom" that had armed and trained the murderers of the Jesuit intellectuals and tens of thousands of others, praising it for having "understood the responsibility that flowed" from power and urging it to continue to put "morality ahead of politics" as it was doing so spectacularly in its traditional domains, and not there alone. The backbone of our actions must be "responsibility," he declared: "responsibility to something higher than my family, my country, my company, my success"—responsibility to suffering people South of the border, in Southeast and West Asia and Africa, and many others like them who could offer direct testimony on the great works of the "defender of freedom." Those that survived, that is, unlike the "voice for the voiceless" silenced by the same defender of freedom to open the decade of vicious terror that Havel found so inspiring, and the six leading dissidents whose voices had been silenced a few weeks before Havel came to Washington to laud the "defender of freedom."[14]

The performance was welcomed with rapture by liberal intellectuals; one might imagine the reaction had the situation been reversed. Havel's soaring rhetoric provided "stunning evidence" that his country is "a prime source" of "the European intellectual tradition" as his "voice of conscience" spoke "compellingly of the responsibilities that large and small powers owe each other," teaching us that we live in a "romantic age" (*Washington Post*, Anthony Lewis, along with a host of others).[15] The responsibilities have since been fulfilled in ways that provide more "stunning evidence" of the "romantic age" in which we have been living for the past decade, now reaching more lofty heights with the new stage of enlightenment and civilization reached in the Balkans.

Havel's "reasoned argument" for bombing was again greeted with acclaim, though not quite with the fervor of the reaction to his ode to those responsible for blowing out the brains of dissident intellectuals, among other exploits. At the outer limits of dissidence, Anthony Lewis was again moved and persuaded by the argument that Havel had "eloquently stated," which eliminates all residual doubts about the nobility of Washington's cause and the "landmark in international relations" that it signals.[16] Others too were overcome by the power of the reasoning.

We may put aside until later the argument (offered by Havel and repeated by Lewis and others) that the nobility of the cause is revealed by the fact that NATO has no "territorial designs" on the Balkans or concern for its resources, an argument that reveals truly "stunning evidence" of failure to comprehend the reasons for military intervention, past and present.

Other moral leaders also enlisted in the cause, among them Elie Wiesel, who was sent to visit refugee camps in Macedonia, Administration officials said, "to focus attention on the moral argument that they say underpins NATO's bombing campaign." A spokesperson for the U.S. Embassy explained that "You need a person like Wiesel to keep your moral philosophy on track." Kosovo is a "moral war," Wiesel affirmed: "When evil shows its face, you don't wait, you don't let it gain strength. You must intervene."[17]

Sometimes, at least. Wiesel has remained faithful to his guiding principle that silence is obligatory in the face of ongoing atrocities, however enormous, if they are carried out by an approved agent. On this matter, he has been forthright. Thus he informed the Israeli press that he had been given documentation (from the Israeli press) by a fellow Nobel Laureate on Israel's critical role in implementing horrendous atrocities in Guatemala, as a U.S. proxy, at a time when direct U.S. engagement was hampered by congressional oversight and public opinion. The documentation was accompanied by a suggestion that he might use his prestige and contacts to keep "evil from gaining strength" to a level that many regard as genocidal. Asked about the matter in an interview in Israel, Wiesel "sighed," the journalist reported, saying that "I usually answer at once, but what can I answer to him?" Not that the documentation is flawed, because he recognized that it was not, but because even private communication exceeds the limits of subordination to state power and violence to which "The Prophet from New York" is committed.[18]

Wiesel's dedication to silence extends to the past as well. Thus he resigned as chair of a (non-governmental) 1982 Tel Aviv conference on genocide at the request of the government, which did not want to anger its Turkish ally by inclusion of the Armenian genocide in the historical survey. The well-known Holocaust historian Yehuda Bauer later informed the press that he had withdrawn from the conference—"a very serious error" he had come to believe—under pressure from the Israeli Foreign Office and after receiving "a telephone call from Elie Wiesel from New York urging me not to participate."[19]

It is understandable, then, that as the war began,

the White House invited a small clutch of guests to join Elie Wiesel, the Holocaust survivor and Nobel Prize recipient, in an East Room discussion on millenial issues. There, where Theodore Roosevelt's children once romped indoors on their ponies, the Clintons listened to the Boston University scholar deliver an address called "The Perils of Indifference" and then lead a conversation about the nexus between morality and politics[20]

—as in Guatemala, Lebanon, and the occupied territories, indeed almost everywhere that the moral truisms mentioned earlier highlight the perils of indifference. One may surmise that these were not the focus of discussion, and that it remained within the bounds of the art that is practiced with great skill by approved moralists, as can readily be determined.

Theodore Roosevelt is introduced because "Clinton has reclaimed the moral power he admired" in his eminent predecessor, aided by Wiesel's wise and principled counsel. Praise of Clinton commonly adduces the TR model, for example, the inspirational words of Secretary of Defense William Cohen, introducing the President at Norfolk Naval Air Station for his first major address a week after the bombing began. Cohen opened by quoting Theodore Roosevelt, speaking "at the dawn of this century, as America was awakening into its new place in the world." In TR's own words: "Unless you're willing to fight for great ideals, those ideals will vanish." And "today, at the dawn of the next century, we're joined by President Bill Clinton" who understands as well as his admired model that "standing on the sidelines…as a witness to the unspeakable horror that was about to take place [in Kosovo], that would in fact affect the peace and stability of NATO countries, was simply unacceptable."[21]

One has to wonder what must pass through the mind of someone invoking this famous racist fanatic and raving jingoist as a model of "moral power" and "American values," even recalling the cause that illustrated his cherished "great ideals" as he issued the ringing declaration quoted: the slaughter of hundreds of thousands of Filipinos who had sought liberation from Spain, shortly after Roosevelt's own contribution to preventing Cubans from achieving the same goal.

Another common argument is that while we "should be pushing intelligently for gains on human rights wherever they can be sought—without of course, making things worse," in sharp contrast we must react with extreme violence in Kosovo (incidentally, "making things worse," by a large factor) "because it *is* in Europe, a Europe essentially occupied for fifty years by our own unilateral security organization, NATO. Kosovo is happening, so to speak, on our watch."[22] Whatever merit the argument has, it holds *a fortiori* for atrocities that are within NATO itself, and under the formal jurisdiction of the European Council and the European Court of Human Rights, which, as noted, continues to issue judgments against those responsible for terrible crimes—the *local* responsible party, not the "defender of freedom" that leads the enlightened states, conducting the atrocities at long-distance in this case. U.S.-supported ethnic cleansing and barbarity in Turkey is most definitely "on our watch," and should be a prime concern, far more so than atrocities in a region that is not part of NATO at all, for the elementary reasons mentioned earlier: our responsibility, and the corresponding ease of mitigating or terminating the atrocities.

Another attempt at exculpation is the observation that Milosevic was not compelled to respond to the NATO bombing with massive atrocities. That is entirely true. By the same logic, we bear no responsibility if we hand guns to acknowledged murderers and then beat them to a pulp, threatening worse, provoking them to carry out the murders that we anticipate. After all, they could have responded by thanking us for our kindness.

Perhaps there are other arguments, but if so, I have been unable to find them in the torrent of words that accompanied the decision to bomb. Perhaps the events really are "a landmark in international relations." It is unusual for the resort to violence to be supported with argumentation so feeble.

One might conjecture that advocates of the escalation of atrocities in Kosovo recognized at some level that constructing a justification posed some non-trivial problems. That might account for the outburst of virulent race-hatred and jingoism, a phenomenon I have not seen in my lifetime since the hysteria whipped up about "the Japs" during World War II, vermin who must be crushed—unlike the Germans, fellow humans who had strayed.

From the outset, Washington understood that "the demonization of Milosevic is necessary to maintain the air attacks."[23] In conformity with this stand, strikes against civilian targets were interpreted as "Raids on Serb Elite's Property." For example, the attack that destroyed the Zastava automobile plant, whose director was a Milosevic associate—the Minister of Privatization, who, we learn in the foreign business press, was an "entrepreneur with no party affiliation [who] was courted by western governments as a leading reformist within the Serbian government and a favorite guest on the diplomatic dinner circuit." "The idea," a senior American military officer said, "is to instill fear in those whose economic standing depends on Mr. Milosevic." The plants destroyed also happened to provide the livelihood for thousands of working people, in the case of the Zastava plant, workers who had carried out a major strike with anti-regime undertones. But that was incidental, as long as the struggle was depicted as NATO vs. the demon Milosevic.[24]

As NATO bombing shifted more explicitly to attacking the civilian society directly, it became necessary to modify the propaganda framework, demonizing the people of Serbia, not merely their leader. Recognizing that "depriving Serbia of electricity, and disrupting its water supplies, communication, and civilian transport, are part of the program,"[25] liberal columnist William Pfaff concluded that it is a mistake to describe NATO's war as "being in conflict only with Serbia's leaders," Milosevic and his cronies. "Serbia's leaders have been elected by the Serbian people," Pfaff now pointed out, and however imperfect the elections, "few suggest that the overall result failed to express the will of the Serbian electorate." We should therefore not misdescribe Milosevic as a dictator; he is a true representative of the Serbian people, who must therefore "not be spared a taste of the suffering he has inflicted on their neighbors" (presumably referring to Kosovo, Washington's deal with the criminal at Dayton having called for no such action). They too must now be demonized, not just their elected leader, if the attack on the civilian society is to be portrayed as an exercise of the New Humanism.[26]

Pfaff did not spell out the tactics he recommended, but in the past he has indicated what he may have had in mind. Surveying the wreckage of Vietnam, he concluded that the United States had followed "a reasonable strategy," but it was "the strategy of those who are rich, who love life, and fear 'costs'." "We want life, happiness, wealth, power," but we failed to comprehend "the strategy of the weak," who "deal in absolutes, among them that man inevitably suffers and dies." Like life itself, the "happiness, wealth, power" that we value are "a dimension of our experience beyond that of the Asian poor," who "stoically accept the destruction of wealth and the loss of lives," inviting us to carry our "strategic logic to its conclusion, which is genocide." But we balk, unwilling to "destroy ourselves...by contradicting our own value system."[27]

The message seems clear: destruction and massacre are "reasonable" as long as they do not reach the level of literal genocide, which would be unacceptable, because we would be "destroying ourselves" if we went that far. Presumably the same moral values hold for the New Humanism. Pfaff did not provide the sources for his insights into the mentality of the Asian poor, but whatever they were, they are no doubt still available to serve current requirements.

At first, Pfaff had directed his "moral outrage" primarily against Milosevic, whose actions demonstrate that "he possesses a moral imagination that merits his comparison with Hitler and Stalin. He acts on a grand scale."[28] Like others who draw the comparison, Pfaff did not go on to raise the obvious questions about those who pursued "a reasonable strategy" in Indochina, stopping short of actual genocide it is true, but surely organizing and conducting atrocities on a far "grander scale" than the demon who compares with Hitler and Stalin. Another of those topics that "it wouldn't do to mention."

It is interesting to see how easily these—after all, fairly obvious—questions are kept unmentionable when Milosevic's actions are portrayed as "wholly comparable with Hitler's and Stalin's forced deportations of entire ethnic groups" (Timothy Garton Ash).[29] The common comparison opens the doors beyond the post-Cold War period to which we are restricted when evaluating the

New Humanism, and should therefore entitle us to ask where we are to rank Washington's "forced deportations of entire ethnic groups" in Indochina, for example. Say in Cambodia, where a million and a half were driven to Phnom Penh alone in the early 1970s. Or the estimated ten million South Vietnamese who underwent "forced deportations" under intensive bombardment and ground sweeps after John F. Kennedy escalated the war in South Vietnam from large-scale state terror to outright aggression in 1961–62.[30] And other examples near and far. If Milosevic's actions are "wholly comparable" to Hitler's and Stalin's, then we must have been mistaken in ranking these monsters so high in the scale of criminality of this terrible century—an extraordinary conclusion that clearly follows from the doctrine set forth with regard to Serbia, though it would be instructive to see it drawn explicitly.

Given the need for collective demonization to justify the attack on the civilian society, it was predictable that Daniel Goldhagen would be called upon to support the thesis that our quarrel is with the Serbs themselves, not just their leader. It is "Milosevic's Willing Executioners" whose deep-seated cultural diseases must be cured. Proponents of the thesis emphasized "especially, the silence of intellectuals on the matter of war crimes" (Stacy Sullivan).[31] That silence is particularly shocking to Western intellectuals, whose "normal world," we are to understand, takes for granted the moral responsibility of devoting itself to the crimes for which they share responsibility, and accordingly could easily bring to an end—the moral truisms mentioned earlier, with the crucial corollary.

Again, it "wouldn't do to mention" the practice of the "normal world" concerning crimes of war and crimes against humanity that are traceable to Washington, London, and other centers of enlightenment. Illustrations can be found at Sullivan's home institution (Harvard's Kennedy School), the journal for which she was a correspondent (*Newsweek*), and the one in which she writes, among many others—in fact, throughout the range of respectable institutions. The journal in which the article appears, for example, is not content with "silence" about terrible crimes, but strongly advocates them, at least in U.S. client states. Thus the editors gave "Reagan & Co. good marks" for their contributions to state terror as it peaked in El Salvador in 1981, and surveying the carnage three years later advised that we must send military aid to "Latin-style fascists…regardless of how many are murdered," because "there are higher American priorities than Salvadoran human rights."[32] The journal's support for Israeli state terror and crimes, and even accusations that extensive reports in the U.S. and Israeli press and TV are "simply not true,"[33] have been too ludicrous to merit comment.

The next logical step in the process was the call to "cleanse Serbia," duly issued in a lead article of the *New York Times* "Week in Review" by Blaine Harden, under the headline "What it Would Take to Cleanse Serbia."[34] The goal of the "cleansing" would be to "stamp out the disease" and "eradicate extreme Serb nationalism," preferably by outright military occupation as after World War II. Particularly obnoxious is "the surreal sense of victimhood in Serbia," "nothing new" in that diseased culture, Harden observes. He quotes Goldhagen, who concludes that "Serbia's deeds are, in their essence, different from those of Nazi Germany only in scale," again opening the highly improper question as to where U.S. crimes must rank, a question barred by "the silence of intellectuals on the matter of war crimes" of their favored states. Like Pfaff, Harden reminds us that Milosevic is "an elected leader," with "soaring popularity in the wake of NATO bombing" (a phenomenon unknown in the West, we are apparently to assume; during the bombing of London, for example). Hence it is the Serbs as a people that must be "cleansed." The call had already been sounded elegantly by the leading *Times* intellectual, Thomas Friedman:

> Like it or not, we are at war with the Serbian nation (the Serbs certainly think so), and the stakes have to be very clear: Every week you ravage Kosovo is another decade we will set your country back by pulverizing you. You want 1950? We can do 1950. You want 1389? We can do 1389 too.[35]

The call to "cleanse" Serbia is particularly appropriate in the United States, a country that is founded on the principle of ethnic cleansing, and that is unusual if not unique in that it has always celebrated the success of the founders in carrying out "the task of felling trees and Indians and of rounding out their natural boundaries,"[36] an achievement that has by no means receded into forgotten history. If the Luftwaffe were to name its attack helicopters "Jew" and "Gypsy," or if the champion college football team in Germany were called "the Munich Kikes," there might be stirrings of disapproval. But one will have to search assiduously for a false note that might disturb the "silence of intellectuals" concerning that very practice in the leader of the enlightened states.[37]

To appreciate the culture of the enlightened, it suffices to ask how many Apaches, Comanches, ... one finds wandering around the country that was once their home, perhaps 10 million of them before the "ethnic cleansing" operations now commemorated in this grisly manner, or how many wielders of tomahawks one finds. We may also remind ourselves that the mascot of the college football champions is the gang of "runaway niggers and lawless Indians" who had to be exterminated—in self-defense, according to the gentlemen honored as heroes (John Quincy Adams, Thomas Jefferson, etc.), who, incidentally, used the opportunity to take Florida from Spain and to establish the doctrine of Executive War in violation of the Constitution, instituting a convention now established by "custom and practice." The "surreal sense of victimhood" that calls for "cleansing" of Serbia (Harden) is a core element of the national culture of the enlightened who are to carry out the cleansing operation, a reflex perhaps of three centuries of highly successful violence.[38]

The picture is even uglier, if that can be imagined. The "new generation" Comanche helicopters, like the Black Hawks that have been employed so effectively in ethnic-cleansing operations within NATO in the 1990s, are manufactured at the Sikorsky plant in Stratford, Connecticut. Sikorsky was bidding to sell Comanches to Turkey even before they were ordered by the U.S. Army. That too seems appropriate. Stratford is the site of the first major slaughter undertaken to cleanse the Northeast region, the Pequot massacre of 1637, still celebrated in children's textbooks as recently as thirty years ago. There the Puritans followed God's command, in their own triumphant and self-congratulatory rendition, by "smiting" the Canaanites and driving them from the Promised Land with a predawn raid while most of the men were away, slaughtering women, children, and old men in Biblical style so that the remnants fled in terror and "the name of the Pequots (as of Amalech) is blotted out from under heaven, there being not one that is, or (at least) dare call himself a Pequot," the conquering heroes proclaimed. That is also the announced intent of the ethnic cleansing operations in Turkey that are to be expedited with the latest Sikorsky killing machines dispatched from the home of enlightenment.[39]

The Founding Fathers knew exactly what they were doing. The first Secretary of War wrote that the English colonists were carrying out "the utter extirpation of all the Indians in most populous parts of the Union" by means "more destructive to the Indian natives than the conduct of the conquerors of Mexico and Peru." Well after concluding his own great contribution to the project, John Quincy Adams became an outspoken critic of both slavery and "the utter extirpation of all the Indians"—policies that he described as "among the heinous sins of this nation, for which I believe God will one day bring [it] to judgement," perhaps judging the contemporary mode of celebration of the sins as well. Adams hoped that his belated stand might somehow aid "that hapless race of native Americans, which we are exterminating with such merciless and perfidious cruelty."[40]

Throughout, the ethnic cleansing operations were conducted with the highest moral values. A classic description was given by Alexis de Tocqueville, who watched the U.S. Army driving Indians from their homes "in the middle of winter" in a "solemn spectacle" of murder and degradation, "the triumphal march of civilization across the desert." He was particularly struck that the conquerors could deprive people of their rights and exterminate them "with singular felicity, tranquilly, legally, philanthropically, without shedding blood, and without violating a single great principle of morality in the eyes of the world." It was impossible to destroy people with "more respect for the laws of humanity," he wrote.

When the task of cleansing the continent was completed, the conquerors proceeded on the same course in the Philippines, also "in the name of humanity" and "in fulfillment of high public and moral obligations." The cleansing operations continue until the present, on a grand scale, sometimes by direct U.S. violence as in

Southeast Asia, sometimes through proxies as in Central America, sometimes for general reasons of state as in NATO during the Clinton years, but always with full "respect for the laws of humanity," and leaving a record that has no blemish, apart from occasional "mistakes" with "good intentions," or such high crimes as the failure to move directly to a ground war in Kosovo.

No high U.S. official has expressed the slightest regret for the Vietnam war, except that it harmed Americans. We owe no debt to the Vietnamese, human rights president Jimmy Carter observed, and have no responsibility to render them any assistance, because "the destruction was mutual." No well-bred American protested, or even thought the statement significant enough to merit comment. Nor was it considered noteworthy when George Bush magnanimously informed the Vietnamese that we threaten no "retribution" for the crimes they committed against us, but only seek honest answers to the single moral issue that remains unresolved in Indochina: the remains of American pilots shot down in self-defense, yet another illustration of the "surreal sense of victimhood" that calls for cleansing of Serbia.[41]

To be precise, traditional U.S. policy is not "ethnic cleansing." Any victims will do, not only those identified by race, religion, color, or other characteristics. The commitment is to ecumenical cleansing. In fact, it is official policy, given the name "counterinsurgency" or "low-intensity conflict."

The enlightened states are well qualified, by culture and by history, to return to their traditional task of "cleansing" the unworthy. In fact it is their qualifications for this task that offer the most powerful mode of denial and evasion. Admiration for leaders and their noble works has been a staple of intellectual discourse from the days of the flatterers at the court in the earliest recorded history, particularly after the successful use of force, which commonly elicits special praise for the leader who is "occupying the moral high ground."[42]

Praise for the peculiar qualifications of the enlightened becomes particularly urgent when it is difficult to conjure up arguments to justify their exercise of force. It is precisely then that one should expect to read about the "moral imperative" that guides the good works of "a society that puts individual freedom first, nourishes a humanitarian ideal, and depends on the cultivation of certain necessary virtues," indeed "the exercise not just of the necessary virtues but of the noble virtues too." A society so exalted cannot "tolerate massive outbreaks of savagery and suffering that are within our power to halt or at least substantially diminish." We are impelled by our very nobility to uphold "the standards our politics teaches us to regard as universal. Kosovo is such an occasion."[43]

That Kosovo is such an occasion has been eloquently proclaimed by Havel, Wiesel, and other moral guides, saluting the leaders of the center of world power. Do these proclamations fall within the tradition of the flatterers of the court for millennia? Or are they really justified in this case, the conjunction of praise and power being mere coincidence? The question is readily answered. It suffices to explore the record of calls for upholding our noble and universal standards in ways that might be harmful to the perceived interests of the powerful to whom we offer allegiance, an inquiry that proves to be not very taxing.

The comparison of our noble selves to the miserable others contributes greatly to the task of demonstrating the virtue of whatever today's cause may be. After all, we live in a "normal world" that is constantly astonished by "the human capacity for evil," foreign to our "custom and practice." "We want life, happiness, wealth, power," and cannot comprehend the mentality of the creatures who "stoically accept the destruction of wealth and the loss of lives," inviting us to commit genocide, though we stop just short, unwilling to "destroy ourselves."

Similar thoughts have sometimes led to skepticism about undertaking the noble cause. Henry Kissinger, for example, believed on such grounds that intervention would be not only a mistake (open-ended, quagmire, etc.), but even futile: "Through the centuries, these conflicts [in the Balkans] have been fought with unparalleled ferocity because none of the populations has any experience with—and essentially no belief in—Western concepts of toleration." At last we understand why not just Americans, but Europeans generally, have treated each other with such gentle solicitude "through the centuries," and have tried so hard "through the centuries" to bring to others their message of nonviolence, toleration, and loving kindness. In his academic essays, Kissinger had probed more deeply into the difference between Us and Them, identifying "the deepest problem of the contemporary international order" as "the difference of philosophical perspective" that separates the West, which "is deeply committed to the notion that the real world is external to the observer," from "cultures which have escaped the early impact of Newtonian thinking" and still believe "that the real world is almost completely *internal* to the observer"—peasants planting their crops, for example, under the delusion that the rain and sun are within their heads (the Russians had begun to grasp the insight, Kissinger explains, though still only in a limited way).[44] Perhaps that even explains the failure of the Vietnamese to submit to the logic of gradual escalation; they thought that the bombings were just a headache, and preferred aspirin to the submission that was anticipated in our "normal world."

Others too ponder "Balkan logic" as contrasted with the record of humane rationality of the "normal world" of the enlightened West. Historians remind us of the "distaste for war or for intervention in the affairs of others" that is "our inherent weakness," and of our dismay over the "repeated violations of norms and rules established by international treaty, human rights conventions" by the disorderly miscreants of the world. Kosovo is "A New Collision of East and West," a *New York Times* think-piece is headlined, illustrating Samuel Huntington's "Clash of Civilizations": the image of "a democratic West, its humanitarian instincts repelled by the barbarous inhumanity of Orthodox Serbs," is "clear to Americans" but not to others, a fact that Americans must learn to comprehend along with the "deeply sobering lessons about the human capacity for evil" that come as such a shock in the centers of enlightenment.[45]

The division between Us and Them became a chasm as the war came to an end, and "Americans, flush with victory over Communism and inhumanity, think ever more reflexively that their values are the world's." But wrongly: "Two Views of Inhumanity Split the World, Even in Victory," we learn from the headline of the featured story of the *New York Times* "Week in

Review."[46] There are still more "deeply sobering lessons" that Americans have to learn. They must come to recognize that not everyone

> shares the West's view that Kosovo is a turning point away from eth-
> nic blood baths and toward harmony, even at Western gunpoint.
> Quite the opposite: the war only underscored the deep ideological
> divide between an idealistic New World bent on ending inhumanity
> and an Old World equally fatalistic about unending conflict.

Regrettably, some fragments of the fatalistic Old World are still able to glance at how the "idealistic New World" is "ending inhumanity" within the territory of its NATO ally, and its client states, and elsewhere in its domains, a flaw that keeps the Old World from fully attaining the heights achieved by the political and intellectual leaders of the idealistic state bent on ending inhumanity. And worse yet, some renegade elements might even remain unconvinced that the idealistic New World was bent on ending inhumanity in Kosovo, or that it did so.

But such strange thoughts should not intrude into our more normal world. Rather, we must come to recognize the "yawning gap between the West and much of the world on the value of a single life." We must face the troubling fact that "a lot of people…just don't buy into Western notions of rights and responsibilities." We may then be able to understand the behavior of Russia, where "ethnic cleansing and forced migration are not exactly unknown" in its history, particularly the pogroms that "forced 1.5 million Russian Jews to flee at the turn of the century." Nothing remotely similar can be imagined in our history, or recent practice. It surely "wouldn't do to mention" that the Kishinev massacre, the most horrendous of the pogroms that forced Russian Jews to flee, was virtually duplicated by the U.S. client regime that devastated much of Lebanon, though all of these crimes pale in comparison to far worse ones that remain properly hidden from inspection and memory.[47]

The correct story, recounted here with zeal, is that the "idealistic New World" has always attached high value to each "single life," though "it took World War II to change the West's mind about inhumanity"—"the West" being Britain, Germany, and

France—"and fifty years more to make that change of mind a commitment." But the Russians are "roughly where Britain, Germany and France were eighty-one years ago," and the rest are too far behind even to begin to grasp the humane values that we have always upheld, now perhaps joined, at last, by some Western Europeans.[48]

It follows without argument that our cause, whatever it is, *must* be just. How can angels be wrong? It would be an insult to offer argument and evidence to justify their behavior, so the topic can be dispatched to its traditional place. Meanwhile we can contemplate the wonderful new era that lies ahead, now that others, at least a few, have joined us in crossing this "landmark in international relations" in a triumph of the human spirit.

Many others have extolled "the universal principles and values espoused by [European Union] and NATO leaders," though with dismay because these principles and values are "lost in the popular discourse of the street," where there seems to be no real appreciation of the mission of "moral intervention" (Tony Blair) when, for "the first time in modern history,...human rights outweighed the sovereignty of state borders" (Vaclav Havel)[49]—unlike the termination of the crimes of the Khmer Rouge by the "Prussians of Asia," or the rescue of Bangladesh by India's advance troops of Russian "hegemonism," or other acts by people still untouched by Western enlightenment.

Only the most unkind will remark that we have heard this before—many, many times—and still await the indication that the magnificence of the conquerors will reveal itself by meeting the only test that has the slightest significance: by undertaking some act from which they do not expect to gain, some genuine "humanitarian intervention" for example. Simple tests are easy to find, right at this moment. Few outside the realms of enlightenment are holding their breath in anticipation for tomorrow's demonstration that the New Humanism differs from the old.

CHAPTER 5

The Diplomatic Record

As noted, the indictment of Milosevic and associates by the War Crimes Tribunal on Yugoslavia was considered to be a "devastating" setback to the ongoing diplomatic process by "Western capitals," though the reports seem conflicting. When the decision to indict was announced on May 27, a court official said that "In effect, this decision has pulled out the rug from under the negotiating process." From Belgrade, Steven Erlanger reported that news of the indictment "stunned Serbs tonight, dampening hopes for an end to the war," particularly because of the timing: the indictment was issued by the (independent) court on the day that Russian special envoy Chernomyrdin "is due here to discuss a peace settlement." The indictment "will greatly complicate" Chernomyrdin's efforts, Erlanger observed. An additional complication was NATO's decision to select the day of the indictment and Chernomyrdin's planned arrival in Belgrade to conduct "the heaviest bombing raids yet on Yugoslavia."[1]

The pattern comes as no particular surprise. It is common, and understandable, for those who monopolize power and the means of violence to use their weapons more intensively as they enter the diplomatic arena, by their own choice or other circumstances: the negotiations to end the Indochina war and the Central America wars of the 1980s are pertinent illustrations, to which I will briefly return.

Chernomyrdin reacted to the increased bombing with an unusually harsh statement.[2] He forcefully rejected Clinton's contention that "Russia is now helping to work out a way for Belgrade to meet [NATO's] conditions" and that NATO's strategy strengthens U.S. relations with Russia. On the contrary, "the new NATO strategy, the first practical instance of which we are witnessing in Yugoslavia, has led to a serious deterioration in Russia-U.S. contacts," which have been set back "by several decades." The intensified bombing, specifically targeting the civilian society, has also radically shifted Russian opinion, reducing the numbers positively disposed toward the U.S. from 57% to 14%. Russians have lost their view of the United States as a model "worthy of emulation," and regard it as having "lost its moral right to be regarded as a leader of the free democratic world." He warned of grim consequences if events proceed on the current course. He also expressed his confidence that China and India were among those who agreed with the Russian stance, rightly it appears. From the hints that have trickled through media and commentary it seems that they are not alone, and that the international community is uneasy about the actions of the enlightened states, or appalled by it, another reflection of the great divide that separates the "idealistic New World" with its occasional associates from the "disorderly miscreants."

Let us review the diplomatic record, asking how it reached the stage that Chernomyrdin and Clinton depicted in their differing ways.

The bombing was undertaken, primarily under U.S./U.K. initiative it appears, after the FRY delegation refused to accept the Rambouillet (Interim) Agreement. There had been discord within NATO, captured in a *New York Times* headline that read: "Trickiest Divides Are Among Big Powers at Kosovo Talks." One problem had to do with deployment of the OSCE monitors. The European powers wanted to ask the Security Council to authorize the deployment, in accord with treaty obligations and international law. Washington, however, refused to allow the "neuralgic word 'authorize'," the *New York Times* reported, though it did finally permit "endorse." The Clinton Administration "was sticking to its stand that NATO should be able to act independently of the United Nations." A leading strategic analyst explains that "To require the Security Council's blessing would essentially hand them a veto over our policy," as articulated in the U.N. Charter.[3]

Discord within NATO continued. Apart from Britain (by now, about as much of an independent actor as the Ukraine was in pre-Gorbachev years), NATO countries appeared to be skeptical of Washington's preference for force, and annoyed by Secretary of State Albright's "saber-rattling," which they regarded as "unhelpful when negotiations were at such a sensitive stage," though "US officials were unapologetic about the hard line."[4]

Current knowledge of diplomatic interactions is thin.[5] Even crucial elements of the record that are fully available remained unreported, including the provisions of the Rambouillet Agreement, finally presented to Serbia and the FRY as "take-it-or-get-bombed" ultimatum, hence of no validity under international law—the discredited old-fashioned kind that is, from which we are now at last to break free, so that we can do what we "believe to be just." But the terms of the Agreement were not made available to the general public. To understand what happened, it is important to find out what they were.

The Rambouillet Agreement called for complete military occupation and substantial political control of Kosovo by NATO, which regards Kosovo as a province of the FRY, and effective military occupation of the rest of the FRY at NATO's will.[6] NATO is to "constitute and lead a military force" (KFOR), which "NATO will establish and deploy" in and around Kosovo, "operating under the authority and subject to the direction and political control of the North Atlantic Council (NAC) through the NATO chain of command"; "the KFOR commander is the final authority within theater regarding interpretation of this chapter [Implementation of the Military Agreement] and his interpretations are binding on all Parties and persons."[7] Civil affairs are to be monitored and supervised by the (NATO-dominated) OSCE and its Chief of Implementation Mission, in coordination with KFOR, the NATO force occupying Kosovo; coordination with an occupying military army is a polite term for subordination. Within a specified and brief time schedule, all Yugoslav army forces and Ministry of Interior police are to redeploy to "approved cantonment sites," then to withdraw to Serbia, apart from small units assigned to border guard duties with limited weapons (all specified in detail). These units would be restricted to defending the borders from attack and "controlling illicit border crossings," and would not be permitted to travel in Kosovo apart from these functions.

"Three years after the entry into force of this Agreement, an international meeting shall to be convened to determine a mechanism for a final settlement for Kosovo." This paragraph has been construed as calling for a referendum on independence, though that is not specifically mentioned.

With regard to the rest of Yugoslavia, the terms for the occupation are set forth in Appendix B: Status of Multi-National Military Implementation Force. The crucial paragraph reads:

> 8. NATO personnel shall enjoy, together with their vehicles, vessels, aircraft, and equipment, free and unrestricted passage and unimpeded access throughout the FRY including associated airspace and territorial waters. This shall include, but not be limited to, the right of bivouac, maneuver, billet, and utilization of any areas or facilities as required for support, training, and operations.

The remainder spells out the conditions that permit NATO forces and those they employ to have free access to the territory of the FRY, without obligation or concern for the laws of the country or the jurisdiction of its authorities, who are, however, required to follow NATO orders "on a priority basis and with all appropriate means." NATO personnel are required to "respect the laws applicable in the FRY...," but with a qualification that renders the condition vacuous: "Without prejudice to their privileges and immunities under this Appendix."

It has been speculated that the wording was designed so as to guarantee rejection. Perhaps so. It is hard to imagine that any country would consider such terms except in the form of unconditional surrender.

In the massive U.S. coverage of the war I found no report of these terms that was near accurate, notably the crucial article of

Appendix B just quoted. The latter was reported as soon as it had become irrelevant to democratic choice on the part of the general public: immediately after the peace agreement of June 3. The press then reported that under the annex to the Rambouillet Agreement "a purely NATO force was to be given full permission to go anywhere it wanted in Yugoslavia, immune from any legal process." Under the "take it or leave it" Rambouillet plan, Guy Dinmore reported in London, "Nato-led troops would have had virtually free access across Yugoslavia, not just Kosovo."[8]

Evidently, in the absence of clear and repeated explanation of the basic terms of the Rambouillet Agreement—the official "peace process"—it was impossible for the public to have any serious understanding of what was taking place.

A few weeks later editorial opinion came to regard the (unreported) Rambouillet Agreement as "so fatally flawed that it helped precipitate what it was meant to prevent—the ethnic cleansing of Kosovo." The editors retrospectively regard the entire proceedings as "a blatant diplomatic failure." "A smarter diplomatic approach that kept the monitors of the Organization for Security and Cooperation in Europe [OSCE] on the ground and engaged the two sides in a genuine political negotiation might have prevented much of the Kosovo catastrophe," but "brute force prevailed over diplomatic skills that might have won the day."[9]

Perhaps some day it will also be recognized that the assumption about what the Agreement and bombing were "meant to prevent" requires argument, not simply repeated assertion, argument that is not so easy to construct in the light of the known facts. And it might even be possible to ask whether the "diplomatic failure" was not the rationally chosen course that led to a predictable victory for the values that mattered, with the fate of the populations an incidental concern, as consistently in the unmentionable past.

The Serbian National Assembly responded to the U.S./NATO ultimatum on March 23. Its Resolution rejected the demand for NATO military occupation, and called on the OSCE and the U.N. to facilitate a peaceful diplomatic settlement. As noted, the Resolution condemned the withdrawal of the OSCE Kosovo

Verification Mission, ordered on March 19 in preparation for the bombing five days later.

The National Assembly Resolution calls for negotiations leading "toward the reaching of a political agreement on a wide-ranging autonomy for Kosovo and Metohija [the official FRY name for the province], with the securing of a full equality of all citizens and ethnic communities and with respect for the sovereignty and territorial integrity of the Republic of Serbia and the Federal Republic of Yugoslavia." Furthermore, though "The Serbian Parliament does not accept presence of foreign military troops in Kosovo and Metohija,"

> The Serbian Parliament is ready to review the size and character of the international presence in Kosmet [Kosovo/Metohija] for carrying out the reached accord, immediately upon signing the political accord on the self-rule agreed and accepted by the representatives of all national communities living in Kosovo and Metohija.

The essentials of the Resolution were reported on major wire services and therefore certainly known to every news room. Several database searches have found scarce mention, none in the national press and major journals.[10]

At a March 24 State Department press briefing, spokesperson James Rubin was asked about the Serbian Assembly Resolution, specifically its reference to an "international presence." Rubin said only that "I'm not aware that anybody in this building regarded it as a silver lining." He seemed not to know what "it" was. Perhaps it was considered insignificant, which would make sense if the point was to send the bombers.

This part of Rubin's press briefing was also apparently not reported; nor, to my knowledge, was the FAIR Action Alert (distributed to the major press) reporting the press briefing.[11]

As to what "it" meant, the answers are known with confidence by fanatics—different answers, depending on which variety of fanatics they are. For others, there would have been a way to find out the answer: namely to explore the possibilities. But the U.S./U.K. and their allies preferred not to pursue this option; rather, to bomb, with the anticipated consequences.

The conventional picture is that "Milosevic's refusal to accept...or even discuss an international peacekeeping plan [namely, the Rambouillet Agreement] was what started NATO bombing on March 24."[12] The term "peacekeeping plan" is used conventionally to refer to whatever plan the U.S. happens to be advocating. The concept "international" also requires qualifications. This article is one of the many deploring Serb propaganda—accurately no doubt, but with some oversights.

Departing from convention, we can conclude that on March 23 there were two peacekeeping plans on the table, both unknown to the general public: the Rambouillet Agreements and the Serb National Assembly Resolution. We can also add a further dimension to the belated recognition that the Rambouillet Agreement was "so fatally flawed" that it "helped precipitate...the ethnic cleansing of Kosovo" (see note 9). When the final decision was made to bomb on March 23, there were two peace proposals, each "fatally flawed," but with a measure of agreement that might have opened the doors to "engage the two sides in a genuine political negotiation [that] might have prevented much of the Kosovo catastrophe." Might have, that is, were such an outcome intended. It took no unique "diplomatic skills" to understand that, merely a willingness to inspect the two plans that had been presented, an option denied to the American people, since both were concealed (and one still is) until it was far too late for them to interfere with the critical choices made by their leaders.

The episode is reminiscent of others, including some within the permitted time frame. A case in point is what took place in the months leading to the bombing of Iraq to expel it from Kuwait in January 1991. From shortly after Iraq's invasion in August 1990, sources in Washington were leaking Iraqi proposals for a negotiated withdrawal that they regarded as "serious" and "negotiable," including an early January proposal that State Department Middle East experts regarded as "a serious prenegotiation position," which Washington "immediately dismissed," and which happened to conform closely with American opinion, as revealed by polls taken right before the bombing. With efficiency that is remarkable in a free society, they were kept from the public eye.[13]

The next important step in the Balkans diplomatic process took place on April 22, at a well-publicized meeting between Milosevic and Washington's favorite Russian, Viktor Chernomyrdin. The meeting was reported, with such headlines as "Russian Ends Peace Visit: Slight Signs of Progress"; "US, Britain reject Serb offer for UN Kosovo role." Chernomyrdin announced that Milosevic had agreed to an "international presence in Kosovo under United Nations auspices" to implement a political settlement and had agreed in principle to "the possibility of an international presence led by the UN" if NATO calls off the bombing. The press reported that "US and NATO officials saw little more in Milosevic's apparent agreement with Chernomyrdin…than the first signs of hope that the Yugoslav president's defiance may be dissolving amid the NATO assault." A post-Peace Accord chronology described the April 22 events as "the first sign of a crack in the Yugoslav position" as Milosevic is reported to be ready to accept an "international presence" in Kosovo, but "alliance officials insist that the bombing won't stop until Belgrade accepts a Nato-led peacekeeping force to protect returning refugees." Regarding Milosevic's "progress" as insufficient, the U.S. and U.K. instantly rejected the proposal and stepped up the bombing of civilian targets (TV was knocked off the air that day).[14]

In brief, on April 22 Milosevic reiterated the proposals of the Serbian National Assembly of March 23, this time in a way that was impossible to evade: namely, via the Russian envoy who is a Western favorite. Since the March 23 proposal had yet to surface, except very marginally, it was possible to present the reiteration of it as a sign that violence works and Milosevic's "defiance" is crumbling under NATO pressure. Therefore more violence is needed.

At another meeting a week later, Chernomyrdin reported "solid progress"—"Hints at Progress," the headline stated. The hint was Serbia's repetition of the National Assembly Resolution of March 23, now amplified to "a U.N. international mission, unarmed and civilian."[15]

The same day, the *Times* published a UPI interview with Milosevic in which he called for a "political process" and said that "The U.N. can have a huge mission in Kosovo if it wishes," a "U.N.

peacekeeping force" with "self-defense weapons," but not "an occupation" of the sort demanded in the "Clinton Administration diktat" at Rambouillet: 28,000 troops occupying Kosovo with heavy equipment. Milosevic also called for reduction of Yugoslav forces to the pre-bombing level of 10–11,000, "return of all refugees, regardless of their ethnic or religious affiliation," "free access for United Nations High Commissioner for Refugees and the International Red Cross," and continuing negotiations for "the widest possible autonomy for Kosovo within Serbia."[16]

Quoting the last phrase, the *Times* reported that Milosevic was "borrowing language from the proposed Rambouillet accords." More significantly, he was repeating the language of the unmentionable March 23 National Assembly Resolution calling for "a political agreement on a wide-ranging autonomy" for the province. Milosevic's April 30 proposals were within the general framework of the March 23 Resolution, with some further detail.

The next phase of the drama took place on May 6, when the Group of Eight (G-8, the major Western countries and Russia) issued an official statement, reported with considerable fanfare. It called for an "immediate and verifiable end of violence and repression," withdrawal of (unspecified) "military, police and paramilitary forces," "Deployment in Kosovo of effective international civil and security presences, endorsed and adopted by the United Nations," "a political process toward the establishment of an interim political framework agreement providing for a substantial self-government for Kosovo, taking full account of the Rambouillet accords and the principles of sovereignty and territorial integrity of the Federal Republic of Yugoslavia and the other countries of the region," and the demilitarization of the KLA.

The G-8 statement was the first step towards compromise between the two plans that were on the table on March 23. It modified the Serb Parliament proposal by the important addition of "security presences," and it abandoned the central demands of the Rambouillet ultimatum on military and political control of Kosovo. The G-8 statement made no mention of NATO and called for "Establishment of an interim administration for Kosovo to be decided by the Security Council of the United Nations...," previously barred from any role by Washington.[17]

The outcome was portrayed as a victory for the U.S./U.K. and a vindication of their resort to force. The lead headline in the *Times* read: "Russia in Accord on Need for Force to Patrol Kosovo." Two stories follow. One opened by saying that "The Clinton Administration...managed to get the Russians on its side today," the second with the words: "The West and Russia agreed for the first time today on the need for an international military presence in Kosovo to keep any eventual peace." "The accord also intensifies pressure on" Milosevic, now isolated, the Russians having come "on board." Veteran *Boston Globe* correspondent John Yemma reported that the primary achievement "was to bring Russia over to the NATO position" on an "international security force" to replace Serb forces, though "before the bombing stops" Milosevic "will have to accept the G-8 plan, at least in principle."[18]

Serbia made no official comment but the Government-run newspaper "printed the set of principles on the front page."[19] The U.S. reacted by dismissing the wording of the G-8 proposal and continuing to insist upon its earlier stand, interpreting developments as an indication that recalcitrants were coming "on board," though not sufficiently, so bombing must continue.

When Yugoslav officials announced that they would accept the outlines of the G-8 plan and called for a Security Council Resolution based on them, NATO reiterated its commitment to the bombardment, stating that "there will be no relief until Yugoslavia accepts the non-negotiable demands of the international community." NATO spokesperson Jamie Shea stated that Milosevic "has begun to move from a position of almost total defiance of the international community when we started [air strikes] to at least now saying that he accepts the key demands of the G8, which embody NATO's five conditions." General Clark added: "I think it's the bombing that is impelling the diplomacy." The bombardment that day hit a crowded bridge, a sanatorium, and a convoy of European journalists.[20]

There was little notice of a letter from Yugoslav Foreign Minister Zivadin Jovanovic to German Foreign Minister Joschka

Fischer which "reiterated that Yugoslavia is now accepting the terms set down weeks ago by the G-8 nations for peace." The letter, released by Germany on June 1, stated that "it is necessary immediately to end the NATO aerial bombardment and to concentrate on a political agenda aimed at reaching a stable and long-lasting political settlement," repeating that the FRY "has accepted G-8 principles, including a United Nations presence, mandate and other elements to be decided by a United Nation's Security Council resolution in accordance with the U.N. Charter."[21]

On June 3, the Kosovo Peace Accord was accepted by NATO and Serbia. On June 8, G-8 agreed on a draft Security Council Resolution to implement the Accord.[22]

There are two versions of the Accord and the U.N. Resolution: (1) the texts, and (2) the U.S./NATO interpretation. As is commonly the case, they differ. Let us consider first the texts (using the text of the Accord provided by the State Department), then turning to the interpretation.

As might have been expected, the Accord is a compromise between the two peace plans of March 23.

The U.S./NATO abandoned their major demands, cited above, which had led to Serbia's rejection of the ultimatum: full military occupation and substantial political control of Kosovo by NATO, and free NATO access to the rest of the FRY. Nor is such access authorized for the security force planned for Kosovo. The Rambouillet wording that has been interpreted as calling for a referendum on independence is also missing.

Serbia agreed to an "international security presence with substantial NATO participation," the sole mention of NATO.

With regard to Kosovo, political control is not to be in the hands of NATO, the OSCE, or Serbia, but of the U.N. Security Council, which will establish "an interim administration of Kosovo." Military control is to be exercised by the "international security presence" which is to be deployed "under U.N. auspices," with "unified command and control," not further specified. The withdrawal of Yugoslav forces is not specified in the detail of the Rambouillet Agreement, but is similar, though accelerated. The remainder is within the range of agreement of the two plans of March 23.

An addendum to the text, not included in either the State Department or the Serb Parliament version, stated "Russia's position [that] the Russian contingent will not be under NATO command and its relationship to the international presence will be governed by relevant additional agreements."[23]

The outcome as of June 3 suggests that diplomatic initiatives could have been pursued on March 23, averting a terrible human tragedy with consequences that will reverberate in Yugoslavia and elsewhere, and are in many respects quite ominous. A diplomatic solution seemed a likely prospect at the outset from inspection of the two peace plans then public (in principle, not in reality), and finally came to be recognized publicly at least in some establishment circles a few weeks later (see note 9).

To be sure, the situation in June is not that of March 23. A *Times* headline the day of the Kosovo Accord captures the prevailing circumstances accurately: "Kosovo Problems Just Beginning." Among the "staggering problems" that lie ahead, Serge Schmemann observed, are the repatriation of the refugees "to the land of ashes and graves that was their home," and the "enormously costly challenge of rebuilding the devastated economies of Kosovo, the rest of Serbia and their neighbors." He quotes Balkans historian Susan Woodward of the Brookings Institution, who points out "that all the people we want to help us make a stable Kosovo have been destroyed by the effects of the bombings," leaving control in the hands of the KLA. Recall that Washington's condemnation of the KLA as a "terrorist group" when it began to carry out organized attacks in February 1998 appears to have been taken by Milosevic as a "green light" for the severe repression that led to the Colombia-style violence prior to the NATO bombing, which precipitated a sharp escalation to the levels that Washington helped create within NATO itself in the mid-'90s.

These "staggering problems" are new. They are "the effects of the bombings" and the vicious Serb reaction to them, though the problems that preceded NATO's resort to force were daunting enough.

The Security Council Resolution, adopted with no significant change of the draft, incorporates the G-8 agreement of May 6 that was accepted by Serbia (Annex 1), and the Kosovo Peace Accord of June 3 (Annex 2). The former makes no mention of NATO; the latter mentions NATO only as noted above. The Resolution itself does not mention NATO, and essentially reiterates the general terms of the Kosovo Peace Accord.

In reporting the U.N. draft resolution, the *New York Times* referred several times to a "footnote on NATO's participation in the security force" that was missing from the Security Council Resolution and from the version of the Accord approved by the Serbian Parliament. Not mentioned is that it was also omitted from the State Department text of the Accord published by the *Times*. Whatever the status of the missing footnote, we again have to distinguish text from interpretation. The text states that:

> It is understood that NATO considers an international security force with 'substantial NATO participation' to mean unified command and control having NATO at the core. This in turn means a unified NATO chain of command under the political direction of the N.A.C. [North Atlantic Council]...NATO units would be under NATO command.[24]

The wording essentially reiterates terms of the Rambouillet agreement cited above, and differs radically from the text of the Accord provided by the State Department and accepted by Serbia, though it presumably does express what "NATO considers." Within a few days, the missing footnote had been reshaped to transmute what "NATO considers" into fact: "What was missing from the final draft was a footnote to the earlier accord that spells out how the security force has 'NATO at the core.' A key sentence describing this as meaning 'a unified NATO command' was also missing."[25]

As fact was translated to more satisfactory interpretation, the press hailed the grand victory of the enlightened states and their leaders. The *New York Times* front-page summary of the "Key Points" of the Accord listed "The establishment of a peacekeeping force led by NATO." Finally "Milosevic Yields on NATO's Key Terms," the front-page headline read, forced "to finally accept

NATO's conditions." Thanks to the Accord, "NATO's peacekeeping force, known as KFOR, will ultimately occupy the entire province," "what will amount to NATO's occupation of Kosovo." Particularly significant was Milosevic's "accepting NATO command" in the NATO-occupied province. NATO spokesperson Jamie Shea "said NATO's command was clear." The Accord guarantees "a single force with a single chain of command," under NATO. News reports exulted that Milosevic had been compelled to submit to a "NATO-led force," "accepting a deal that was not even as good for him as the one he could have had" before the bombing "laid waste to his country," though "Western nations are considering new arrangements to military command to ease Russia's concerns about its place in the NATO-led security force in Kosovo.[26]

In passing, we might note that Shea's daily performances as (British) spokesperson for NATO follow a well-trodden track, pioneered during World War I by the British Ministry of Information, which secretly defined its task as "to direct the thought of most of the world"—primarily the thought of American intellectuals, whose help was needed to whip a pacifist population into jingoist war fever and was offered with great success according to their own self-congratulatory judgment.[27] Shea may well have been following that model consciously. He is a "clever student of what he refers to as 'mass persuasion techniques'," the *Washington Post* reported in a profile after the war ended, and the "author of a doctoral thesis on the role of European intellectuals in marshaling public opinion in favor of the First World War..."[28]

The profile goes on to report Shea's file of "headhunters who have telephoned over the past two months with lucrative private-sector opportunities," offers he may take up "before the tan begins to fade." If so, he will follow a tradition that has had an enormous impact on 20th-century life. The huge public relations and advertising industries, the "political warfare" conducted by the British Conservative Party to fend off the rising threat of democracy, and the projects of "manufacturing consent" recommended and implemented for the same ends by the self-described "responsible intellectuals" were shaped quite consciously by the successes of the

Anglo-American state propaganda agencies. Several of their participants went on to achieve much fame and influence (notably
Walter Lippmann, the dean of American journalism and a highly
respected commentator for half a century, and Edward Bernays, one
of the founders of the Public Relations industry).

The *New York Times* editors warned Washington to "guard
against" a weak Security Council Resolution, "insuring that a
Kosovo-resolution closely adheres to the peace plan" of June 3,
which "means among other things that peacekeeping forces operate
under a NATO chain of command"; "overall command must be
retained by Western nations," though "it would be best" to allow
Security Council authorization "to eliminate the perception that
[the peacekeepers'] presence is solely an American or NATO operation." Other reports emphasized the main lesson of the war:
"Bombing Can Work." Bombs and missiles compelled Milosevic to
"capitulate," to "say uncle" and accept "NATO's terms."[29]

On June 10, the Security Council Resolution was adopted in
accord with the draft already discussed, mandating a force with
NATO participation under U.N. auspices. Under the headline
"Security Council Backs Peace Plan and a NATO-led Force,"
Judith Miller reported that the Security Council approved a
Resolution "sending a large NATO-led force into Kosovo," a
Resolution that "bestows United Nations legitimacy on the peace
plan and the NATO-led military operations in Kosovo."[30]

Not quite what the texts say, but a story that is far more useful
than the facts. With the story firmly in place, efforts to keep to the
actual texts will become "Russian defiance of NATO" and "Serb
trickery and deviance." Unilateral U.S.-NATO imposition of their
own rules will count as strict adherence to the accords they are violating. So matters played out in the days that followed, and presumably will continue to do so in a world governed by force, with the
meaning of words determined by power.

The only serious issue debated was whether the outcome shows
that air power alone can achieve the highly moral purposes to
which the enlightened states are dedicated, or whether, as critics
allowed into the debate allege, the case has yet to be proven.
Speaking for the critics, the editors of the *Boston Globe* conceded

that they had been wrong while Clinton and the NATO command were proven right. The results demonstrate that "airpower alone could carry the day,...even if it failed to protect 1.5 million uprooted Kosovars"—"uprooted" as a consequence of the bombing, as predicted and later acknowledged, but better forgotten. A leading liberal columnist exulted that NATO leaders "won their bet" that "air power alone would defeat Milosevic," who "started the whole thing, driving one million ethnic Albanians from their homeland"—after the bombing that he had ardently supported. Many others reiterated the same themes, with general agreement that as a result of NATO bombing Milosevic "surrendered as close to unconditionally as anyone might have imagined."[31]

"John Keegan, the highly regarded military historian and defense editor of The Daily Telegraph in London, admitted gracefully last week that he had been wrong in saying...that air power alone could not win the war," Anthony Lewis wrote in his paean "When Praise is Due," hailing Clinton's triumph. At the dissident left extreme of admissible opinion, only one question is conceivable: Are the tactics employed by the powerful successful? Sometimes they are seen to be inadequate, as in Vietnam, when a year and a half after Wall Street ordered an end to a war that it had come to perceive as too costly, Lewis admitted gracefully that although the U.S. had intervened with "blundering efforts to do good"—another thesis that is true by definition, requiring no evidence—"by 1969" it had become "clear to most of the world—and most Americans—that the intervention had been a disastrous mistake," "that the United States had misunderstood the cultural and political forces at work in Indochina—that it was in a position where it could not impose a solution except at a price too costly to itself." That was always the argument against the war, he explained. Hence it is unnecessary to attend to the opinion of a large majority of the public that the war was not "a mistake" but was "fundamentally wrong and immoral," a position that has, remarkably, held steady into the late 1990s without any support from articulate opinion.[32]

The majority opinion is uninterpretable within the framework of elite opinion. The figures are therefore interpreted as showing a "preference to avoid undertaking major burdens in foreign interventions," a completely different matter but one that is at least compatible with received ideology.[33]

Keegan is indeed a knowledgeable and respected military historian, and it is worthwhile to read what he said:

> The air forces' victory in the Balkans is not just a victory for Nato or for the "moral cause" for which the war was fought. It is a victory for that New World Order which, proclaimed by George Bush in the aftermath of the Gulf war, has been so derided since…If Milosevic really is a beaten man, all other would-be Milosevics around the world will have to reconsider their plans, [recognizing] that there are now no places on Earth that cannot be subjected to the same relentless harrowing as the Serbs have suffered in the past six weeks. What that implies, it may be judged, is that no rational ruler will choose to commit the crimes that have attracted such punishment. The World Order looks better protected today than it did the day before the bombing began.

At the time of the Gulf war, Keegan had explained why England is such a willing participant in Washington's crusades. "The British are used to over 200 years of expeditionary forces going overseas, fighting the Africans, the Chinese, the Indians, the Arabs. It's just something the British take for granted," and the war in the Gulf "rings very, very familiar imperial bells with the British"—as does the style of the wars, at least for those who do not prefer "intentional ignorance."[34]

Keegan's observations are astute, but require some commentary and translation. This is by no means the first time that air power has been used to "bomb the niggers" into submission. As British military historians at least must be aware, the famous victory of 1999 vindicates the strategy that Britain pioneered after World War I with no little success: reliance on air power and poison gas to subdue the "recalcitrant Arabs" and other "uncivilised tribes" who aroused Winston Churchill's ire (poison gas had already been used by British forces in their invasion of Russia, quite successfully according to the British High Command).[35] It is true, however, that the means available then were primitive, and no doubt modern technology has overcome many of those deficiencies.

Keegan's assessment may be realistic, if we interpret the goals and significance of the New World Order in the terms elaborated in an important documentary record of the '90s that remains largely out of sight (see chapter 6), and a plethora of factual evidence that helps us understand the true meaning of the phrase "Milosevics around the world." Merely to keep to the region near Kosovo, the strictures do not hold of huge ethnic cleansing operations and terrible atrocities within NATO itself, under European jurisdiction and with decisive and mounting U.S. support, and in this case not a brutal response to an attack by the world's most awesome military force and the imminent threat of invasion. Such crimes are legitimate under the rules of the New World Order, perhaps even meritorious, as are atrocities elsewhere that conform to the perceived interests of dominant sectors in the enlightened states, and are regularly implemented by them when necessary. Such facts, not particularly obscure if we escape the protection of "intentional ignorance," reveal that in the "new internationalism...the brutal repression of whole ethnic groups" will not merely be "tolerated," but actively expedited—exactly as in the "old internationalism" of the Concert of Europe, the U.S. itself, and many distinguished predecessors.

We return to how "World Order looks" from outside the enlightened states—and from within, from the perspective of top planners.

Others also pondered broader themes. "NATO's air strikes may have changed forever the old rules of war," Philip Stephens reflected.[36] That is a curious comment from a British analyst, who can hardly be unaware of Britain's record of "reserving the right to bomb niggers," and should have no difficulty in understanding why the press in the former British colonies, when they were carrying out mass murder in the Philippines, recommended that U.S. forces continue "slaughtering the natives in English fashion" so that "the misguided creatures" who resist us will at least "respect our arms," and later come to recognize that we wish them "liberty" and "happiness."[37] The laws of war remain those of European civilization, not without analogues and predecessors.

Some expressed concern about the KLA, to be "demilitarized" but not disarmed, high officials explained, a distinction that is a little obscure, since they are only lightly armed. The question whether they could become "a benign police force" rather than one that "vexes NATO" was addressed by correspondent John Yemma, relying on his experience in the Middle East. The best hope would be for the KLA to "transform itself from a guerrilla army into a peacetime security force, much as the Palestine Liberation Organization has done."[38] Yemma is offering a model that has been bitterly and uniformly condemned by international, Israeli, and Palestinian human rights groups for its violence, torture, terror and repression, "creating a climate of fear and intimidation"[39]—but this time in a worthy cause, in service to Washington's "peace process" for Israel-Palestine. The Wye Agreement of October-November 1998, which advanced the U.S.-Israeli program of effective takeover of the occupied territories, may be the first international agreement on record that virtually mandates the resort to state terror and severe human rights abuses to ensure security for the part of the population that matters. It was, accordingly, hailed with awe, while Clinton was praised as the "Indispensable Man" who is "staking out the moral high ground" in the "uplifting, optimistically American" style, "tethering the vaunted American idealism."[40]

Those who have paid attention to the evolution of the "peace process" that the U.S. imposed will be aware that the model recommended now for Kosovo is itself modelled closely on the functions and behavior of the Black police of the South African "homelands" in the worst days of Apartheid thirty-five years ago. That much at least seems clear enough, whatever one thinks about Washington's Israel-Palestinian "peace process."

Returning to the Kosovo Peace Accord, one might argue that the media and commentators are realistic when they present the U.S./NATO version as the facts. Whatever the discrepancy between Washington's version and the texts, the former is likely to prevail as a simple consequence of the distribution of power and the willingness of articulate opinion to serve its needs. In particular, the discrepancy between the Rambouillet Agreement and the Kosovo Peace Accord will be resolved by force, the essential terms of Rambouillet becoming the operative terms of the Accord: on the ground, in commentary, and probably in history. The Accord and the Security Council Resolution confirming it place military and political control over Kosovo in the hands of the United Nations, but these terms are unacceptable to the rulers. We can be confident that the outcome will be the Rambouillet demand that NATO occupy the territory under the military and political control of the North Atlantic Council, and maintain effective control of civilian affairs as well, whatever the soothing words may say.

The phenomenon is routine. It received a classic literary expression centuries ago when Pascal, in his satire on casuistry, singled out the "utility of interpretations" as the most effective mechanism by which the powerful can loftily uphold high principles while reversing them in practice. A cruder version in modern totalitarian states was labelled "Newspeak" by Orwell.[41] It is familiar in practice, including pertinent recent examples in Indochina and Central America, where diplomatic initiatives were instantly reversed by force.

The apparent use of force to deter or shape diplomacy was discussed during the Indochina wars.[42] The practice rose from apparent to transparent with the Paris Peace Treaty of January 1973, which was to bring the wars to an end. In October 1972, an agreement had secretly been reached by the U.S. and North Vietnam, but Washington withdrew its consent, blaming Vietnam. The Christmas bombings of December 1972 were undertaken to coerce Hanoi to abandon the October agreement and settle for terms more to Washington's liking. When that tactic failed, the U.S. agreed to approximately the same terms in January 1973, though only formally. Kissinger and the White House announced at once, quite lucidly, that they would violate every significant element of the Peace Treaty they had now agreed to sign, presenting a completely different version of its terms. The latter was adopted in reporting and commentary.

The U.S. quickly resorted to substantial violence to reconstitute the Treaty in terms more to its own liking. When the Vietnamese enemy finally responded to serious violations of the Treaty by the U.S. and its client regime, Hanoi was depicted with much indignation as the incorrigible aggressor that had to be punished once again. With pretexts shifting as circumstances dictated, severe punishments were administered in the years that followed throughout Indochina, until today, and the versions imposed by power have successfully displaced the facts in the intellectual culture. The story is a triumph of the "utility of interpretations."[43]

The tragedy/farce was re-enacted during the Central American wars of the 1980s. The Reagan Administration sought to undermine repeated diplomatic efforts to resolve the conflicts, a procedure often described by government and press as "promoting the peace process." The need to undermine a peaceful settlement became acute when the Central American Presidents agreed on the Esquipulas Accord (the so-called "Arias plan") in August 1987, over strong U.S. opposition. Washington at once escalated its wars in violation of the one "indispensable element" of the Accord; with impunity, thanks to media cooperation. Simultaneously, it proceeded to dismantle the other provisions of the Accord by force and threat, succeeding within a few months. The Accord was dead by January 1988, replaced by a U.S. version. Washington continued to undermine further diplomatic efforts by the creatures in the "unimportant places" until its final victory throughout the devastated region. Washington's version of the Accord, which deviated from it sharply in essential respects, became the accepted version. The outcome could therefore be heralded in headlines as a "Victory for U.S. Fair Play" with Americans "United in Joy" over the ruins and bloodshed, while columnists gushed that "we live in a romantic age," all reflecting the general euphoria over a mission accomplished.[44]

Another relevant example already mentioned is Israel's U.S.-backed invasion of Lebanon in 1982, undertaken to deter the threat of a diplomatic resolution that might interfere with U.S.-Israeli plans to integrate the useful parts of the occupied territories within Israel. The matter was widely discussed from the outset by Israeli scholars, political leaders, and commentators. It is, however, off the record in the more disciplined leader of the free world, where the prevailing version is that the U.S. client state was defending itself from international terrorism.[45]

It is superfluous to review the aftermath in these and numerous similar cases. There is little reason to expect a different story to unfold in the present case—with the usual and crucial proviso: If we let it.

The ink was hardly dry on the Kosovo Peace Accord before the traditional methods went into operation. NATO announced that it "will step up bombing" because of Serbian efforts to evade "non-negotiable" demands presented by NATO officials, while "Serbs Balk Over Details" and "Serbs seen pressing for role by UN," head-lines read. "Pointedly, [the Deputy Foreign Minister of Yugoslavia] said Yugoslavia interpreted the agreement to require 'deployment of an international security presence under auspices of the U.N. or a presence established under a Security Council Mandate'." Another way to present the facts would be to say: "Pointedly, Yugoslavia insisted on the actual wording of the Kosovo Peace Accord, which called for 'Deployment in Kosovo under U.N. auspices of effective international civil and security presences acting as may be decided' by the U.N. Security Council, rejecting 'nonnegotiable' NATO demands that conflict with the Peace Accord that the U.S. has declared irrelevant." The proper version is that Milosevic is "pos-turing" and trying to "buy time" when Yugoslav generals attempt to "hand over control of the Serbian province to the United Nations rather than NATO," deceitfully calling for observance of the Accord that was signed and therefore "pressing for role by UN," rather than following the orders from on high.[46]

A follow-up is headlined "Tricky Point for Serbs: No Mention of U.N. Role." The implicit assumption is that it is not a tricky point for the U.S. and its media, because the official agreements, which not only "mention the U.N. role" but place it at the core of the process, are just another scrap of paper, as demonstrated by Washington's instant dismissal of the documents it signed—yet another display of the traditional contempt of the powerful for solemn treaties, the United Nations, and institutions of world order generally. Hence the Serbs are "stalling" when Serb negotiators "balked at the absence of any reference to a United Nations role in the peacekeeping forces for Kosovo," unwilling to agree to the six-page "nonnegotiable" NATO demands that were "distilled" from the Kosovo Peace Accord—namely, by replacing its core provisions with NATO's contrary demands.

As correspondent Elizabeth Becker rightly observed, "However the politicians resolve the United Nations issue, NATO will command" the peacekeeping force. True enough, and another demonstration of the principle of the New Humanism, as of its distinguished predecessors: the world is ruled by force, under a veil of moral purpose woven by the educated classes, who, as throughout history, preach eloquently about "a landmark in international relations," a "new era" of justice and righteousness under the courageous leadership of the enlightened states, by accident their own.[47]

"Stalling" and deceit appear to be a trait of Slavs generally, not just Serbs. The Russians too were reported to be "balking," holding up the U.N. Resolution that assigns political and military control to the Security Council. Russian "balking" is their insistence "that the United Nations have some role in peacekeeping" as required by the Kosovo Accord and the Resolution—to be more accurate, the leading role in peacekeeping. But unlike the Serbs, the Russians are not all bad: "Still, the Russians helped secure the agreement with Yugoslavia last week," even though they are disrupting the proceedings with their crude tactic of insisting on the terms of documents that were signed.

A dose of reality was administered by a "senior Administration official" who stated that according to the Resolution, "we're going to have unified command and control" under NATO, with the United Nations nodding its head politely. "The word NATO may not be mentioned in the resolution, an official said, but one section of the draft says the operation will be 'performed by member states and relevant international organizations'." So it does, but with no special role for NATO and with responsibility assigned to the United Nations; and without the "missing footnote" stating that "NATO considers" the agreements "to mean…a unified NATO chain of command under the political direction" of the North Atlantic Council, the terms of Rambouillet that were abandoned by NATO—though only formally. In the real world, as opposed to the world of solemn agreements, "We have already crossed the Rubicon that it will not be run by the United Nations," State Department spokesperson James Rubin instructed. Accordingly, whatever the wording may be, the Resolution calls for "the entry of

50,000 troops under NATO command," John Broder reports under the headline "Optimism, And More Realism, On Talks About Withdrawal."[48]

"Milosevic is trying to cull elements of victory out of defeat," British Defense Minister George Robertson thundered, accusing him of "bad faith" and "procedural trickery," and expressing "American and British outrage over the refusal by Yugoslav military commanders to accept NATO military terms": the "nonnegotiable" demand that NATO will run the occupation of Kosovo, whatever the signed documents say. Russia still "seems to agree" with Serbian efforts to "go back on the agreement," the press reported, referring to Russia's insistence that "The Security Council...is the only institution in charge of scope, modalities and mandate of an international presence" in the FRY, "in line with the political agreement and principles set out in Belgrade" by Finnish President Martti Ahtisaari when he presented the G-8 demands.[49]

It may be true that the Resolution makes no mention of NATO apart from the annex reiterating the Kosovo Accord, but the meaning of both documents is clear, by Washington's diktat. As for the "footnote" to the Kosovo Accord omitted from the Resolution (and from the State Department text of the Accord), its contents were soon upgraded, omitting the phrase "NATO considers," as already illustrated. The "key sentence from the footnote" now is: "This in turn means a unified NATO chain of command under the political control of the North Atlantic Council." In the (omitted) text this is what "NATO considers"; it is now elevated to fact, though the devious Milosevic "could exploit this absence of detail, balking at any measures that were not spelled out in the resolution." A senior NATO official warned that Serbs may not agree to anything "that goes further than the Security Council resolution." As in the days when the Concert of Europe was conducting the civilizing mission, the Serbs remain "Orientals, therefore liars, tricksters and masters of evasion."[50]

Matters proceeded on course as "NATO peacekeeping troops entered Kosovo" on "Chinook helicopters, carrying British and Gurkha paratroopers," to be followed by convoys of heavy equipment and troops. The Chinook/Gurkha reference, without embarrassment or even notice, reflects again the glorification of imperial violence and ethnic cleansing. But "the NATO-led peacekeeping mission approved last week by the United Nations Security Council" had a rude shock, as "Again, a defiant Moscow challenges West," sending a small contingent of troops a few hours earlier. "Alarm was generated today when a senior [Russian] Defense Ministry official...publicly warned that Moscow might unilaterally send troops to Kosovo if NATO did not drop its insistence that it command all the forces there"—that is, NATO's insistence on violating the Peace Accord and the Security Council Resolution. The Russians "backed Belgrade in insisting that the peacekeepers serve under a United Nations flag," in compliance with the formal agreements but in violation of the correct interpretation. The events raised serious questions about "who is in charge" in Russia, and whether the still-dangerous bear will be able to live up to its obligations under the interpretations of the ruling casuists.[51]

In brief, all systems seem to be in place, as expeditiously as one might expect from recent precedents. U.S./NATO demands have become The Facts—which is not, of course, to deny that Serbia will try to play the same game, though lacking the power and means of violence, they cannot succeed any more than others who defy the master.

Quite correctly, the press continues to condemn the Serb "propaganda machine that has aroused public opinion for war in Kosovo" and is now "preparing Serbs for a peace deal." There is a "huge gap between government rhetoric and reality in a society where the news media is state-controlled."[52] True, though two questions are in order:

(1) Could there be a gap between rhetoric and reality in the free societies?

(2) What was the situation in Serbia before the bombing?

Let's put aside question (1) and turn to (2). We find that the gap was very real, though it was considerably reduced by access to foreign radio and TV broadcasts. And before "democracy activism" became "a war casualty," there were also "several opposition newspapers as well as radio and TV outlets," the British Helsinki Human

Rights Group reported, while "numerous anti-Milosevic foreign-funded NGOs also operated in the country," mostly closed down after the bombings. In Kosovo itself, the Albanian separatist press continued to publish openly, along with the Hungarian-language press, through the Rambouillet negotiations in February 1999, reporting Serb atrocities and praising NATO's "readiness to use force" and "to dispatch tanks and infantry to Kosovo," where "Serbia may lose its sovereignty."[53]

It may be useful to recall the performance of the U.S. government and media in wartime, when the U.S. faced no threat of foreign attack at all; or, for that matter, the performance of the most free and democratic of its client states, Israel, far superior to that of the U.S. though still highly repressive, more so, for example, than Nicaragua under severe U.S. attack. It is enlightening to compare reactions in the media and commentary to press freedom in the '80s in the U.S. client states of Central America (where vicious and murderous repression received scant notice), in Israel (highly praised with virtually no report of press repression), and Nicaragua—bitterly condemned while freely allowing publication of the leading journal *La Prensa*, which openly supported the attack on Nicaragua and called for its intensification, behavior unthinkable in U.S. client states or the United States itself even under much less onerous conditions. The matter is so utterly incomprehensible in the enlightened states that it will probably never pass the Orwellian barriers.[54]

The gap between rhetoric and reality in the Serbian media provided the justification for NATO bombing of Serb radio and TV from April 8, finally reducing much of the TV headquarters to rubble with a missile attack on April 23—"on the eve of NATO's 50th anniversary celebration," the *Financial Times* observed. Politely, we continue to avoid the possible implications relating to question (1). NATO military spokesman Air Commodore David Wilby justified the attacks on the grounds that the Serb media were a "legitimate target which filled the airways with hate and with lies over the years," though NATO at first offered to allow the media to "escape further punishment" if Milosevic "gave six hours of air space to western news broadcasts each day," emulating standard practice in the United States.[55]

On similar grounds, NATO forces in Bosnia subjected Serbian Radio Television (SRT) in Republika Srpska—the "ethnic Serb mini-state" within Bosnia—to closure and other coercion. The specific charges were that SRT had omitted thirty seconds of a statement by Madeleine Albright "discussing her warm feelings for the Serbs," "was failing to explain that NATO troops were bombing Yugoslavia to end ethnic cleansing in Kosovo, and was giving the impression that the world opposed the strikes." In short, SRT was refusing to broadcast NATO propaganda that is manifestly false, and was giving impressions that are largely true, though they receive scant notice here. Another charge was that SRT was focusing on the priorities of its audience, Serbs in Bosnia, not those of NATO. In 1997 the European Union's high representative in Bosnia, Carlos Westendorp, had "seized SRT's transmitters" and "turned the station over to politicians who favored better relations with the West," including the director now under attack for insubordination. On April 7, 1999, Westendorp went further, asking NATO to "cut off the offending material at its source" by bombing Belgrade's state television, as it did the next day.[56]

The commitment to control information sources falls within a far more general pattern. A revealing example is the virtual destruction of UNESCO when it began to consider proposals to democratize the international media system to permit some access on the part of the vast majority of the world. That initiative elicited an extraordinary flood of condemnations from the U.S. government and the media, replete with deceit and lies that were reiterated without change after refutation, which was rarely permitted expression. "The stunning irony of this achievement," an academic historian of U.S.-UNESCO relations observes, "was that the United States, having proved that the free market in ideas did not exist, attacked UNESCO for planning to destroy it." A detailed review of media and government deceit was published by a university press, but also ignored. The events provide another instructive measure of the attitudes towards the basic principles of freedom and democracy.[57]

CHAPTER 6

Why Force?

Turning from reasonably well-confirmed and generally uncontested fact to speculation, we may ask why events proceeded as they did, focusing on the decisions of U.S. planners—the factor that must be our primary concern on elementary moral grounds, and that is a leading if not decisive factor on grounds of equally elementary considerations of power.

We may note at first that the dismissal of Kosovar democrats "in deference to Milosevic" is hardly surprising. The pattern is traditional. To mention just some examples within the restricted time frame, after Saddam Hussein's repeated gassing of Kurds in 1988, in deference to its friend and ally the U.S. barred official contacts with Kurdish leaders and Iraqi democratic dissidents (according to their account); they were virtually excluded from the media as well. The ban was officially renewed in March 1991, immediately after the Gulf war, when Saddam was tacitly authorized to conduct a massacre of rebelling Shi'ites in the south and then Kurds in the north. The massacre proceeded under the steely gaze of Stormin' Norman Schwartzkopf, who explained that he was "suckered" by Saddam, not anticipating that Saddam might carry out military actions with the military helicopters he was authorized by Washington to use. The Bush Administration explained that support for Saddam was necessary to preserve "stability;" its preference for a military dictatorship that would rule Iraq with an "iron fist" just as Saddam had done was sagely endorsed by respected U.S. commentators.

Tacitly acknowledging past policy, Secretary of State Albright announced in December 1998 that "we have come to the determination that the Iraqi people would benefit if they had a government that really represented them." A few months earlier, on May 20, Albright had informed Indonesian President Suharto that he was no longer "our kind of guy," having lost control and disobeyed IMF orders, so that he must resign and provide for "a democratic transition." A few hours later, Suharto transferred formal authority to his hand-picked vice president. The democratic transition continued with the June 1999 elections, celebrated as the first democratic elections in over forty years, but with no reminder of why there had been no elections during this period. The reason is that the Indonesian parliamentary system was undermined by a major U.S. clandestine military operation in 1958, undertaken in large measure because the democratic system was unacceptably open, even allowing participation of a political party (the PKI) that "had won widespread support not as a revolutionary party but as an organization defending the interests of the poor within the existing system," developing a "mass base among the peasantry" through its "vigor in defending" their interests. The party was wiped out a few years later, along with hundreds of thousands of landless peasants and other miscreants. The CIA ranked the slaughter alongside the mass murders of Hitler, Stalin, and Mao. The enlightened states greeted it with unrestrained euphoria, praising the "Indonesian moderates" who had successfully cleansed their society, and welcoming them to the Free World, where they retained their high rank until Suharto's first crimes in early 1998.[1]

More marginalia "it wouldn't do to mention" as the "idealistic New World bent on ending inhumanity" has finally enlisted at least some Europeans in its cause.

We need not tarry on the plausibility of Washington's discovery of the merits of democracy in 1998. The fact that the words can be articulated, eliciting no comment, is informative enough. In any event, there is no reason to be surprised at the disdain for nonviolent democratic forces in Kosovo; or at the fact that the bombing was undertaken with the likely prospect that it would undermine a courageous democratic movement in Belgrade, seriously so, as reported immediately and repeatedly since: Serbs are "unified from heaven—but by the bombs, not by God," in the words of Aleksa Djilas, the historian son of Yugoslav dissident Milovan Djilas. "The bombing has jeopardized the lives of more than 10 million people and set back the fledgling forces of democracy in Kosovo and Serbia," Serb dissident Veran Matic wrote, having "blasted…[its] germinating seeds and insured they will not sprout again for a very long time"; Matic headed the independent station Radio B-92 (banned after the bombing), and had just received the Olof Palme award presented by the Swedish Government for exceptional contribution to the development of democracy (January 30, 1999). As already discussed, the bombing had the same effect in the largely dissident region of Vojvodina, far from Kosovo, where it was particularly destructive. Former *Boston Globe* editor Randolph Ryan, who had been working for years in the Balkans and living in Belgrade, wrote that "Now, thanks to NATO, Serbia has overnight become a totalitarian state in a frenzy of wartime mobilization," as NATO must have expected, just as it "had to know that Milosevic would take immediate revenge by redoubling his attacks in Kosovo," which NATO would have no way to stop.[2]

With the basic facts in mind, one may speculate about how Washington's recent decisions were made. Only speculate: direct evidence is slight.

Turbulence in the Balkans qualifies as a "humanitarian crisis," in the technical sense: it might harm the interests of rich and privileged people, unlike slaughters in Sierra Leone or Angola, or crimes we support or conduct ourselves. The question, then, is how to control the authentic crisis.

The conventional approach is to arm and train the state security forces to suppress the unwanted turbulence, as in Turkey, Colombia, El Salvador, and a long list of others. But that method is available only when they are obedient clients. Serbia, whatever one thinks of it, is a last holdout of independence in Europe, hence disqualified for this task. With the standard method ruled out, the next option would be to follow solemn treaty obligations, the "supreme law of the land," and turn to the institutions of world order. But these Washington does not tolerate. The next choice is

NATO, which the U.S. at least dominates. The divisions within NATO are understandable: Washington's primary advantage is its domination of the means of violence, and at a much lower level the same is true of its junior partner. In any confrontation it is natural to play one's strong card, then to see what happens. As to what planners "envisioned," the confidence expressed by Carnes Lord and others is not easy to share. If the record of past actions is any guide, the consequences for people who live in the "unimportant places" were incidental.[3]

Throughout the crisis, NATO leaders emphasized, with general agreement, that the decision to bomb on March 24 was obligatory for two reasons: (1) to stop the violent ethnic cleansing that the NATO bombing precipitated, as anticipated; and (2) to establish "the credibility of NATO." The first reason we may put aside, but the second is plausible.

It is necessary to guarantee the "credibility of NATO," political leaders and commentators reiterated forcefully. "One unappealing aspect of nearly any alternative" to bombing, Barton Gellman observed in a *Washington Post* review of "the events that led to the confrontation in Kosovo," "was the humiliation of NATO and the United States."[4] National Security Advisor Samuel Berger "listed among the principal purposes of bombing 'to demonstrate that NATO is serious'." A European diplomat concurred: "Inaction would have involved 'a major cost in credibility, particularly at this time as we approach the NATO summit in celebration of its fiftieth anniversary'." "To walk away now would destroy NATO's credibility," Prime Minister Tony Blair informed Parliament. Clinton's position was explained by a "White House official":

> From the first day, he said we have to win this. It was absolutely clear. Because of the consequences for the U.S., for NATO, for his responsibilities as Commander in Chief, we had to win this.

"NATO's only alternative, then, was to bomb—a lot," *Times* correspondent Blaine Harden comments in a lengthy retrospective on White House planning.[5]

Another detailed *Times* account of how and why the White House went to war quoted Secretary of Defense William Cohen at a private meeting of NATO defense ministers in October 1998, at a time when NATO was offering mixed reports of responsibility and was interpreting renewed Serb atrocities as a reaction to the takeover of 40% of Kosovo by the KLA during the preceding months of relative restraint. Cohen outlined Clinton's plan for air strikes, and "challenged his colleagues to embrace a new role for the alliance. If NATO could not muster a threat to Mr. Milosevic under these circumstances, he asked, what was the point of the alliance?" Threats to bomb "quickly became a test of NATO's credibility, with the added onus of the alliance's looming 50th anniversary" in late April. Meanwhile diplomacy was "derailed" by miscalculations and distractions resulting from White House scandals.[6]

British military historian John Keegan dismissed the resort to "sentiment" by Blair and others who were "appealing to the sympathies of the British." There is a crisis, but it is "a crisis of credibility for the alliance on which our survival has depended for 50 years." U.S. commentators generally agreed. Thus William Pfaff wrote early on that "the debate about intervention is no longer a dispute over the means to an end. It is a debate over abandoning NATO and the American claim to international leadership": "If there is no NATO victory over Serbia, there will no longer be a NATO," so "the only solution" is for the NATO military "to drive organized Serbian forces out of Kosovo, destroy them and the present Serbian government."[7]

After the Peace Accord of June 3, leaders and analysts recognized that the outcome was not entirely satisfactory, but agreed that there had been one crucial success: "the goal of maintaining NATO credibility was achieved."[8]

To interpret the praise for a job well done, we have to carry out the usual translations. When Clinton, Blair and others speak of the "credibility of NATO," they are not expressing their concern about the credibility of Italy or Norway: rather, of the reigning superpower and its attack dog. The meaning of "credibility" can be explained by any Mafia Don. When a storekeeper does not pay protection money, the goons who are dispatched do not simply take the money: they leave him a broken wreck, so that others will get the message. Global Mafia Dons reason the same way, and understandably so.

It is not, of course, that the Don needs the storekeeper's money. The common argument that this intervention must have been humanitarian because Kosovo has few significant resources or other use for the West reflects a serious misunderstanding of the basic elements of policy and recent history. Did the instant move to undermine the Bishop government in Grenada, and later invade, grow out of concern about the nutmeg trade? Did the U.S. cherish the resources of Guatemala, Indochina, Cuba, Nicaragua, and a long list of other targets of violence in recent years? It is true that in efforts to enlist support, such claims were sometimes made (the tin and rubber of Indochina, etc.), but surely not taken very seriously. And sometimes particular business interests may influence policy (e.g., United Fruit in Guatemala), but rarely as a primary factor. The issues were consistently different.

One persistent concern is to establish "credibility," a requirement that becomes still more urgent if there is a perceived danger that the "rotten apple" might "spoil the barrel," that the "virus" of independence might "infect" others, in the terminology of high-level planners. The concern of the Kennedy intellectuals over "the spread of the Castro idea of taking matters into one's own hands" is a case in point. With adjustments to particular circumstances, such considerations regularly underlie intervention and conflict, and even the Cold War itself from its onset in 1917: Russia was perceived to be a huge "rotten apple," eliciting fears that remained a leading element in Western policy at least into the 1960s, when the Soviet economy entered a period of stagnation from which it never recovered. Resource control and other such interests are often at stake, but rarely in the target of attack itself, at any significant level (with some exceptions, e.g., oil producers, including Indonesia in 1958).

Furthermore, Cold War issues were usually marginal to intervention, which is why the pattern persists with little change before, during, and after the Cold War. Sometimes the fact is emphasized forcefully in the internal record: for example, in 1958, with regard to the three major world crises that Eisenhower and Dulles identified at the National Security Council: Indonesia, North Africa, Middle East, all Islamic, but more significantly, all oil producers. Eisenhower stressed emphatically that there was no Russian involvement, even behind the scenes, the secret record reveals.[9]

It is also understood that violence may not immediately succeed, but planners can be confident that there is always more in reserve. If necessary, the Carthaginian solution is available. Those who are skeptical might take a stroll through large areas of Indochina. The direct targets, and others who may have odd ideas about raising their heads, must come to understand that fact. Hence the need for credibility.

Apart from that consistent fact, there are side benefits to the resort to violence in the Balkans. One has already been mentioned: Serbia was an annoyance, an unwelcome impediment to Washington's efforts to complete its substantial takeover of Europe. Although the resources of the Balkans are of no great interest, their strategic location is, not only with regard to Europe, West and East, but also the Middle East. The first major postwar counterinsurgency campaign, in Greece, was motivated in large part by concern over control of Middle East oil, also a factor in U.S. subversion of Italian democracy in the same years.[10] Greece remained within the Near East section of the State Department until the fall of the U.S.-backed fascist dictatorship twenty-five years ago. Though secondary, similar concerns now extend to Central Asia; and proximity to Turkey, Washington's major military base in the region along with Israel, is also presumably a factor in planning. As long as Serbia is not incorporated within U.S.-dominated domains, it makes sense to punish it for failure to conform—very visibly, in a way that will serve as a warning to others that might be similarly inclined. The 1998 crisis in Kosovo offered an opportunity to do just that, and we can expect with fair confidence that the process will continue until Serbia either succumbs or is crushed, as in the case of Cuba and other recalcitrants.

For the purposes of "population control" at home, different tunes are played, varying with circumstances (tentacle of the Russians, our "yearning for democracy," etc.). But unless firmly dedicated to "intentional ignorance," we can dispense with them.

Another side benefit is the stimulus for military production and sales. "Overall, the war is likely to boost defense spending generally," the *Wall Street Journal* reported, primarily for high technology military systems. Raytheon alone expected about $1 billion in orders to replenish stocks of Tomahawk cruise missiles and other weapons employed "to blast targets in the Balkans." The figure does not include new orders expected from other NATO countries. The "real winners in wars" are military industry, a headline in the *Financial Times* observes. The story reviews the "reasonably buoyant" prospects for aerospace, particularly elements with more sophisticated and expensive technology; half the cost of a new fighter aircraft is avionics equipment and software, hence a boost to the high-tech economy generally.[11]

For the audience of the business press it is unnecessary to spell out the rest of the story. Military spending has been a primary cover for the huge state sector of the high-tech economy, the basis for U.S. preeminence in computers and electronics generally, automation, telecommunications and the internet, and indeed most dynamic components of the economy. The story goes back to the origins of the U.S. system of mass production in the early days of its industrial development, though it only took on enormous proportions after World War II. The role of the state sector was also fundamental for agricultural production, and now extends to the biology-based industries as well, which, like high tech, are reliant on socialization of cost and risk and the economic weapons of state power (for example, to enforce intellectual property rights and other forms of market interference, in the interests of major corporations). With regard to the military cover, the guiding principle was enunciated frankly by Secretary of the Air Force Stuart Symington in January 1948: "The word to talk was not 'subsidy'; the word to talk was 'security'."[12]

The "real winners" go beyond high-tech industry. Major U.S. construction companies (Brown & Root, Halliburton, Bechtel) "have already made clear that they are eager to rebuild roads and bridges" that have been "blasted" by their high tech associates, and Western energy companies are also looking forward to "rebuilding power-distribution networks." The British fear that they may again "miss out," as they did after the Gulf war, displaced by U.S. and continental rivals. The government's Department of Trade and Industry is moving to co-ordinate efforts by British companies to participate in "the reconstruction of Kosovo," a plum roughly estimated to amount to some $2 billion to $3.5 billion over the next three years.[13]

War may be "the Health of the State," as Randolph Bourne observed, but we have to understand "state" in terms far broader than mere governmental functions.

A possible benefit is a more aggressive posture for NATO, a useful outcome insofar as Europe remains under control, not at all a certainty. U.S. planners are surely ambivalent about the decision of the European Union, in the wake of the war, to move towards a "unified defense policy" that will enable it to act independently of the United States in "peacekeeping and peacemaking missions"—"defense" and "peacemaking" being understood under the usual translations.[14]

With that last consideration in mind we may return to military historian/analyst John Keegan's observation that the outcome of the war is "a victory for that New World Order" that was "proclaimed by George Bush in the aftermath of the Gulf war," and that the "World Order looks better protected" after the victory of air power in the Balkans. The latter sentiment was underscored by President Clinton in his victory speech, reporting "to the American people that we have achieved a victory for a safer world."[15]

These assessments are plausible on the tacit assumption that "the world" excludes most of the world. What is protected is the "international community," in the technical sense of the term: rich and privileged sectors in the industrial societies of the West, and their associates and collaborators elsewhere.

Keegan's comments on the Gulf war require a similar gloss. That war too was hailed as a triumph of the "international community," and the grand victory was also accompanied by glowing rhetoric about the promise of a new era of international morality. But as at least a scattering of Western commentators observed, the war policy of the U.S./U.K. left them in a "tiny minority in the world"—the actual world, that is.[16]

The general mood outside the rich industrial societies was captured by Cardinal Paulo Evaristo Arns of São Paulo, Brazil, who wrote in 1991 that in the Arab countries "the rich sided with the U.S. government while the *millions* of poor condemned this military aggression." Throughout the Third World, he continued, "there is hatred and fear: When will they decide to invade us," and on what pretext?

By the time the two warrior states decided to bomb Iraq once again in December 1998, their isolation was far more pronounced. And though they have enlisted some sectors in support of their latest moral crusade, it appears that a large majority of the world's population is asking Cardinal Arns's question.

Even in virtual client states the mood is not exactly euphoric. The semi-official Egyptian press expressed serious concern over the "New Strategic Concept" released at the NATO anniversary in April, as the war in the Balkans raged. Karim El-Gawhary saw it as "a licence for world-wide interventionism." NATO's discovery of "new risks to 'Euro-Atlantic peace and stability'" has an ominous ring to those who have had more than enough experience with European benevolence; it is not only the British who hear "very, very familiar imperial bells" as the U.S./U.K. go on another rampage in the name of virtue. "Seen from the perspective of the Alliance's periphery—for example, from the view of the Arab world—the document reads like a recipe for nightmare," as NATO's concept of defense extends to "security and stability in the Mediterranean," and beyond, reviving a history that is well understood, on the basis of rich experience, outside of the enlightened states that constitute the official "international community."[17]

To be sure, concern over "the flow of vital resources" and "stability" in the approved sense "sounds quite familiar," the *Al-Ahram* analysis continues. As noted, such concerns motivated U.S. intervention in Greece and even Italy in the early postwar years. But "what is so new and so radical about the document" is that, though designed in Washington, "it is signed by all the 18 other NATO member states," so that actions against "any other defiant state on the Euro-Atlantic periphery can now be performed in the name of

NATO," adding another dimension to the U.S. mode of world domination—at least, as long as Europe remains compliant.

Repeating a theme that resonates throughout the "unimportant places," El-Gawhary takes particular notice of the fact that "the UN Security Council, as an instrument to keep the international peace, is only mentioned in the new NATO document for appearances sake," implying that in the future NATO will "increasingly take matters into its own hands," under a strategic concept that "effectively enshrines the right of the powerful to interpret international law to suit their interests." This too "sounds quite familiar," taking its place alongside the entrenchment and expansion of traditional "custom and practice" under the rubric of the triumphalist New Humanism.

In neighboring Israel, former military intelligence officer Amos Gilboa, a respected centrist commentator on military and security affairs, expressed still harsher views of "the foolish initiatives of NATO and the U.S. to establish new rules of the game," though on different grounds. He pointed out realistically that the rules "are likely to accelerate the competition to develop nuclear arms." The reasons are clear. Others will ask the obvious question: "Would NATO have even conceived of bombing Yugoslavia if it knew that Belgrade had access to weapons of mass destruction?" Knowing the answer, they will be tempted to develop a powerful deterrent to protect themselves from the marauding superpower. The "new rules of the game" of the U.S. and its "rich Western allies," as revealed in Yugoslavia, are based on "the right to intervene with force to compel what seems to them to be justified. As in the colonial era, so now as well, the use of force is cloaked in moralistic righteousness." When NATO spokespersons calmly describe their destruction of the civilian society, "it is difficult to believe that the words are coming from the mouths of states that we call 'enlightened'," though the self-designated "enlightened states," to be sure, regard themselves rather differently, as in the colonial era and throughout history. The 20th century is ending with a new kind of "gunboat wars," just as the last century ended with "the war of the colonial powers of the West, with overwhelming technological advantages, subduing natives and helpless countries that had no ability to defend themselves."[18]

For the rest of the world there is "no choice," Gilboa concluded. "They must obtain weapons of mass destruction. The war in Kosovo will yet be revealed as a competition to proliferate weapons of mass destruction," in self-defense.

These analysis are supported by Israel's leading military historian, Ze'ev Schiff. Like El-Gawhary, he writes that "NATO's new thinking," as presented by Tony Blair at the NATO anniversary, "is certain to arouse unease all over the world" because of its disregard for the principles of the UN Charter. The lessons that NATO draws from its military victory "might change international diplomacy and slide into dangerous territory," and might persuade other potential targets "to arm themselves with nuclear weapons in order to 'defend' their acts of cruelty"—or to defend themselves from other projects, such as NATO's "desire to respond to a grave threat against international energy resources," or in fact any other that the global ruler may choose to undertake.[19]

Moving a few steps farther from the "international community," we find that the Indian government also "made known its serious concern over NATO's new doctrine that permits operations beyond the Euro-Atlantic region and outside the territory of the alliance. Any such action, said an official spokesman, would contravene international law, norms of peaceful coexistence between the nations and the U.N. Charter." The government deplored "the increasing tendency of NATO to usurp the power and function of the U.N. Security Council." "The propensity of NATO to extend its areas of operation was seen as a source of concern to all countries, big and small." The official comment also "came close to the strong condemnation by various sections of non-official opinion which saw NATO emerging as a rogue force on the international scene." It expressed once again India's strong opposition to NATO's use of force in Yugoslavia, and reiterated the position of the government from late 1998 that "the problem should be resolved through consultation and dialogue and not by confrontation." On this matter India was in substantial agreement with Russia and China, and, it appears, a good part of the rest of the world, though in the absence of coverage of "unimportant places" little can be said with any confidence.[20]

The *Times of India* was also highly critical of the resort to force "before exhausting the full possibilities of a negotiated settlement." It too warned of "very serious consequences to major nuclear arms control issues." A second major national newspaper, the *Hindu*, condemned NATO for operations "characterized by illegality, self-interest, arrogance and lawlessness," as "NATO is fast displacing the United Nations as the peacekeeper of the world," lending its power "to any country or sect of religion which regards itself as a contemporary ally of America—irrespective of whether or not such action has the official support of the U.N." "We need a machinery to end atrocities against humanity. But, such a system cannot be built around self-interested interventions by America through NATO," actions that are particularly egregious after the U.S. was explicitly "forbidden" to undertake unilateral military intervention by the World Court in the Nicaragua case. The U.S. has become "the rogue state par excellence repeatedly defying international rulings whether by the World Court or by U.N. resolutions when these have not suited its interests," and its current actions lack any "serious or genuine legal, moral, political justification."[21]

The Indian press also called for the U.N. to "assert its authority and take on the direct responsibility" of implementing the Kosovo settlement, in accord with the Security Council Resolution,[22] an option that was quickly dispatched to its usual place as the U.S./NATO imposed their own interpretation on the Accord and the accompanying Security Council Resolution, in the routine manner already discussed.

The concerns of the former colonial world are recognized, and to an extent shared (though from a different perspective), by more perceptive hawkish policy analysts. In the leading establishment journal, *Foreign Affairs*, Samuel Huntington warned that Washington is treading a dangerous course. In the eyes of much of the world—probably most of the world, he suggests—the U.S. is "becoming the rogue superpower," considered "the single greatest external threat to their societies." Realist international relations theory, he argues, predicts that coalitions may arise to counterbalance the rogue superpower. On pragmatic grounds, then, the stance should be reconsidered.[23]

Americans who prefer a different image of their society might have other grounds for concern over these tendencies, but such matters are probably of little interest to planners, with their narrower focus and immersion in ideology.

The matter of nuclear arms is of particular significance with the recent breakdown of the Nonproliferation Treaty in South Asia—that is, what is left of the NPT with the refusal of the nuclear powers to observe "the NPT's stated goal of eliminating nuclear weapons" and their resistance to even "modest proposals for focusing on the implementation of the nuclear disarmament provisions of the treaty."[24]

Concern over these critical issues, alongside the growing wariness about the revived expansionism of the "rogue superpower" and its associates, takes on a still more somber cast in the light of current strategic planning. Some insights are given by a partially declassified 1995 study of the U.S. Strategic Command (STRATCOM), called "Essentials of Post-Cold War Deterrence," reviewing "the conclusions of several years of thinking about the role of nuclear weapons in the post-Cold War era."[25]

The central conclusion is that the reliance on nuclear weapons is to remain fundamentally unchanged, including the rejection of the basic thrust of the NPT, except that the scope of their potential use is broadened beyond the Cold War enemies, now considered to be at least partially tamed. The new target list extends to "rogue" states of the Third World—meaning not murderous and dangerous states, but disobedient ones (e.g., Cuba, or Iraq after Saddam disobeyed orders but not when he was committing his worst crimes and amassing weapons of mass destruction with U.S./U.K. assistance). Israel, for example, is not so designated, because it is considered an appendage of U.S. power, even though in the view of the former Commander in Chief of STRATCOM (1992–94), General Lee Butler,

it is dangerous in the extreme that in the cauldron of animosities that we call the Middle East, one nation has armed itself, ostensibly, with stockpiles of nuclear weapons, perhaps numbering in the hundreds, and that inspires other nations to do so.[26]

The STRATCOM study stresses the need for *credibility*: Washington's "deterrence statement" must be "convincing" and "immediately discernible." The U.S. should have available "the full range of responses," but nuclear weapons are the most important of these, because "Unlike chemical or biological weapons, the extreme destruction from a nuclear explosion is immediate, with few if any palliatives to reduce its effect." "Although we are not likely [sic] to use nuclear weapons in less than matters of the greatest national importance, or in less than extreme circumstances, nuclear weapons always cast a shadow over any crisis or conflict," and must therefore be available, at the ready. One section is headed: "Maintaining Ambiguity." It is important that "planners should not be too rational about determining…what the opponent values the most," all of which must be targeted. "[I]t hurts to portray ourselves as too fully rational and cool-headed." "That the US may become irrational and vindictive if its vital interests are attacked should be a part of the national persona we project." It is "beneficial" for our strategic posture if "some elements may appear to be potentially 'out of control'."

These concepts resurrect the "madman theory" attributed to Richard Nixon, but this time with credible evidence that the theory is in place. Our enemies should recognize that the "rogue superpower" is dangerous, unpredictable, ready to lash out at what "they value most." They will then bend to our will, aware of our "irrationality and vindictiveness" and the destructive force at our command, fearing our "credibility." The concept was apparently devised in Israel in the 1950s by the governing Labor Party, whose leaders "preached in favor of acts of madness," the dovish Prime Minister Moshe Sharett recorded in his diary, warning that "we will go crazy" ("nishtagea") if crossed, a "secret weapon" aimed in part against the U.S., which was not considered a trustworthy godfather at the time. In the hands of the world's sole superpower, which regards itself as an outlaw state and is subject to few constraints from elites within, that stance raises natural concerns among those who do not have the luxury to content themselves with the "cloak of moralistic righteousness" derided by serious analysts.[27]

Nuclear weapons "seem destined to be the centerpiece of US strategic deterrence for the foreseeable future," the STRATCOM report on "Post-Cold War Deterrence" concludes. We should therefore reject a "no first use policy," and should make it clear to adversaries that our "reaction" may "either be response or preemptive." We should also reject the stated goal of the NPT and should not agree to "Negative Security Assurances" that ban use of nuclear weapons against non-nuclear states that are parties to the NPT.

President Clinton did in fact issue a "Negative Security Assurance" in 1995, but it was overridden by the internal "US nuclear posture," as the BASIC study documents (see note 24). A subsequent Clinton Decision Directive of November 1997 leaves Cold War planning on course, apart from the broadening of targets.

A separate paragraph of the STRATCOM study deals with "Creative Deterrence," offering one illustration: when Soviet citizens were kidnapped and killed in Lebanon, "the Soviets had delivered to the leader of the revolutionary activity a package containing a single testicle—that of his eldest son." "Such an insightful tailoring of what is valued within a culture, and its weaving into a deterrence message,…is the type of creative thinking that must go into deciding what to hold at risk in framing deterrent targeting"— against defenseless enemies, as the example illustrates.

The general framework is a shift of "deterrence strategy" as the Cold War ended in November 1989: from Russia and China, to the Third World generally. The shift was signalled in the annual message sent to Congress calling for a huge military budget (March 1990).[28] It was much like earlier requests, apart from the pretexts: not that the Russians are coming, but because of the "technological sophistication" of Third World countries. This new threat requires that we maintain "the defense industrial base" (a.k.a. high-tech industry), and powerful intervention forces. These continue to be aimed primarily at the Middle East, where the "threats to our interests" that have required direct military engagement "could not be laid at the Kremlin's door." Nor could the threats be laid at Iraq's door: Saddam was still a friend and ally.

The phrasing reflects the end of the Cold War. A National Security Directive of October 1989, recommending continued support for Saddam, called for "the use of U.S. military force" where "necessary and appropriate" to defend our "vital interests...against the Soviet Union or any other regional power..." A month before the fall of the Berlin Wall the threat to our interests still could "be laid at the Kremlin's door."[29]

This shift of "deterrence strategy" having taken place, the international environment "has now evolved from a 'weapon rich environment' to a 'target rich environment'," the Defense Special Weapons Agency explained. Russia was "weapon rich," but the South generally is "target rich," with "increasingly capable Third World Threats," the Joint Chiefs of Staff determined in a March 1990 assessment, coinciding with the public message to Congress.[30] Targets are now to include nations capable of developing weapons of mass destruction, a very broad category, including any country with laboratories, industry, and infrastructure. The new "globality capability" is to extend to the region "south of the equator" (metaphorically speaking, I presume). Another innovation is "adaptive planning," to allow rapid action "in response to spontaneous threats" from smaller countries, previously disregarded in nuclear strategy. Technical innovations include "mini-nukes" tailored for use against the disobedient ("rogue nations").

STRATCOM's position is "that the basic role of nuclear weapons in US security policy has not changed with the end of the Cold War." However, "planning for nuclear war with the Third World was a new development," the BASIC study observes, adding that "the United States is sending a message that nuclear weapons are important for achieving prestige in world affairs and for accomplishing military and political objectives," and that the NPT is dead in the water as far as the U.S. is concerned (and probably lesser nuclear powers as well).

The major effect of the end of the Cold War, the BASIC study points out, is that an "important constraint is missing," namely the Soviet deterrent. That was predicted by strategic analysts well before the fall of the Berlin Wall, and has been evident in practice since, even in the invasion of Panama a few weeks later, where the new opportunities were specifically noted by high level officials.[31]

One consequence of the end of the Cold War has been the collapse of the Soviet economy, leaving millions prematurely dead and the society in ruins apart from the wealthy elites linked to foreign power, a natural and predictable effect of the reversion of Russia to its pre-Cold War status as part of the West's "Third World," subordinated to the market principles that the West has preached to deadly effect, for others.[32] The greater freedom for the enlightened states to undertake military adventures follows at once. A related consequence is the collapse of nonalignment, an option when two global Mafia Dons are on the loose, gone when there is only one "rogue superpower." Here other factors contributed, among them the economic catastrophe that swept much of the Third World, affecting the richer countries too, ever since the wave of financial liberalization and a specific form of "globalization" imposed in the interests of the powerful.

With the deterrent removed and Third World independence (nonalignment) reduced to the merest shadow, we should hardly be surprised at the general disregard for Third World interests, evident in a range of policies from nuclear strategy to foreign aid, and also anticipated.[33]

The disdain was starkly illustrated in February 1999, when two important high-level summits took place: the G-7 summit of the rich industrial world, and the G-15 summit, representing such unimportant places as India, Mexico, Chile, Brazil, Argentina, Indonesia, Egypt, Nigeria, Venezuela, Jamaica (where the meeting was held), and others like them.

The G-7 summit was prominently covered, with particular focus on the discussions of a "new financial architecture" to deal with the massive market failures that were becoming a "crisis" in the technical sense—threatening the interests of the rich and powerful, not just everyone else.

The G-15 summit was also concerned with financial architecture, but from a different perspective. The meeting emphasized the need to impose conditions on financial flows so that speculative capital will not destroy economies at will, with the IMF in the background as the "credit community's enforcer" (in the words of the current U.S. executive director of the IMF), ensuring that creditors gain high yields from risky loans but with the risks socialized, borne primarily by the populations of the South under IMF austerity programs, secondarily by Western taxpayers who provide free risk insurance.[34] G-15 participants warned that "unbridled capitalism endangers the very independence of developing countries by leaving them at the mercy of international lending institutions and colossal foreign companies," AP reported. The Secretary-General of UNCTAD (U.N. Conference on Trade and Development, the major U.N. economic research agency) predicted a "bleak future" for the vast majority of the people of the world unless these issues are seriously addressed. The Prime Minister of the host country observed that the traditional double-edged market principles—free markets for the poor, market interference as needed for the rich—"threaten the very economic survival of many countries within the developing world." Others expressed similar fears and concerns.[35]

The likelihood that the issues will be seriously addressed by the enlightened is indicated by the coverage: brief notice in the New York *Daily News*, the *Chicago Tribune*, and the Minneapolis *Star Tribune*.[36] The reasons were clear enough to G-15 participants. They were stated by Malaysian President Mahathir Mohamad:

> Paradoxically, the greatest catastrophe for us, who had always been anti-communist, is the defeat of communism. The end of the Cold War has deprived us of the only leverage we had—the option to defect. Now we can turn to no one.

No paradox, but the natural course of real-world enlightenment, for centuries.

The topic goes well beyond the range of discussion here, but the essential points are quite relevant to the "license for world-wide interventionism" perceived in much of the world, which interprets the Balkans affair and its implications quite differently from the norm of the enlightened states.

Chapter 7

World Order
and Its Rules

"**O**ne accusation rarely noted in the American press, but extensively accepted as truth abroad, was that the bombing of Yugoslavia was a flagrant violation of sovereignty and international law," Serge Schmemann observes at the end of a long lead review article on the consequences of the war.[1] The reasons for the division are readily understood by those who do not indulge in "intentional ignorance," a few examples already cited.

Despite the desperate efforts of ideologues to prove that circles are square, there is no serious doubt that the NATO bombings further undermine what remains of the fragile structure of international law. The U.S. made that clear in the debates that led to the NATO decision, as already discussed. The more closely one approached the conflicted region, the greater in general was the opposition to Washington's insistence on force, even within NATO (Greece and Italy). Again, that is not an unusual phenomenon: another recent example is U.S./U.K. bombing of Iraq, undertaken in December 1998 with unusually brazen gestures of contempt for the Security Council—even the timing, coinciding with an emergency session to deal with the crisis. Still another illustration is Clinton's destruction of half the pharmaceutical production of a small African country a few months earlier, another event that does not indicate that our "moral compass" is straying from righteousness. It was dismissed here as a marginal curiosity, though comparable destruction of U.S. facilities by Islamic terrorists might evoke a slightly different reaction. Perhaps this is an example of the kind of "creative deterrence" advised by STRATCOM, aiming at what "is valued within a culture," such as the fate of children dying from easily curable disease.

It should be unnecessary to emphasize that there is a far more extensive record that would be prominently reviewed right now if facts were considered relevant to determining the "custom and practice" that is called upon to confer upon the most enlightened state the right "to do what it thinks right" by force.

It could be argued, rather plausibly, that further demolition of the rules of world order is by now of no significance, as in the late 1930s. The contempt of the world's leading power for the framework of world order has become so extreme that there is little left to discuss. A review of the internal documentary record demonstrates that the stance traces back to the earliest days, even to the first memorandum of the newly-formed National Security Council in 1947. During the Kennedy years, the stance began to gain overt expression, as, for example, when the eminent statesman and Kennedy advisor Dean Acheson justified the blockade of Cuba in 1962 by informing the American Society of International Law that the "propriety" of a U.S. response to a "challenge...[to the]... power, position, and prestige of the United States...is not a legal issue." "The real purpose of talking about international law was, for Acheson, simply 'to gild our positions with an ethos derived from very general moral principles which have affected legal doctrines'"—when convenient.[2]

The main innovation of the Reagan-Clinton years is that defiance of international law and solemn obligations has become entirely open, even widely lauded in the West as "the new internationalism" that heralds a wonderful new age, unique in human history. As already discussed, the developments are perceived rather differently in the traditional domains of the enlightened states; and, for different reasons, are of concern even to some hawkish policy analysts.

The end of the Cold War made it possible to transcend even Achesonian cynicism. Bows to world order are unnecessary, even to be despised, as the enlightened states do as they please without concern for deterrence or world opinion. Doctrinal management suffices "'to gild our positions with an ethos derived from very general moral principles," as recent developments show with much clarity. "Innovative but justifiable extension of international law"[3] can be devised at will by the powerful, to serve their special interests: "humanitarian intervention" by bombs in Kosovo, but no withdrawal of a huge flow of lethal arms for worthy ethnic cleansing and state terror within NATO itself, to cite only the most dramatic illustration. With "unpopular ideas silenced and inconvenient facts kept dark" in the style described by Orwell in his (silenced) observations on the free societies, all should proceed smoothly. Whatever happens is "a landmark in international relations" as the "enlightened states," led by an "idealistic New World bent on ending inhumanity," proceed to use military force where they "believe it to be just"—or as others see it, to devise "rules of the game" that accord them "the right to intervene with force to compel what seems to them to be justified," always "cloaked in moralistic righteousness," "as in the colonial era" (Gilboa).

From the perspective of the enlightened, the difference of interpretation reflects the sharp divide that separates their "normal world" from that of the backward peoples who lack "Western concepts of toleration" and have not yet overcome "the human capacity for evil," to the astonishment and dismay of the civilized world.

In this context, it is hardly surprising that "international law is today probably less highly regarded in our country than at any time" since the founding of the American Society of International Law in 1908. Or that the editor of the leading professional journal of international law should warn of the "alarming exacerbation" of Washington's dismissal of treaty obligations.[4]

The prevailing attitude towards institutions of world order was illustrated in a different way when Yugoslavia brought charges against NATO countries to the World Court, appealing to the Genocide Convention. The Court determined that it had no jurisdiction, while holding that "All parties must act in conformity with their obligations under the United Nations Charter," which clearly bars the bombing—"veiled language to say that the bombing was breaking international law," the *New York Times* reported.[5] Of particular interest was the submission of the U.S. government, which presented an airtight legal argument, accepted by the Court, that its actions did not fall under Court jurisdiction. The U.S. had indeed ratified the Genocide Convention, after a very long delay, but with a reservation that "the specific consent of the United States is required" if charges are brought against it; and the United States refuses to give the "specific consent" that the reservation stipulates. Court rules require that both parties agree to its jurisdiction, Counsel John Crook reminded the Court, and U.S. ratification of the Convention was conditioned on its inapplicability to the United States. QED.[6]

It may be added that the reservation is more general. The U.S. ratifies few enabling conventions concerning human rights and related matters, and these few are conditioned by reservations that render them (effectively) inapplicable to the United States.[7]

The explanations offered for rejection of international obligations are interesting, and would be on the front pages, and prominent in the school and university curriculum, if honesty and human consequences were considered significant values.

The highest authorities have made it clear that international law and agencies had become irrelevant because they no longer follow Washington's orders, as they did in the early postwar years, when U.S. power was overwhelming. When the World Court was considering what it later condemned as Washington's "unlawful use of force" against Nicaragua, Secretary of State George Shultz—honored as the Mr. Clean of the Reagan Administration—derided those who advocate "utopian, legalistic means like outside mediation, the United Nations, and the World Court, while ignoring the power element of the equation." Clear and forthright, and by no means original. State Department Legal Advisor Abraham Sofaer explained that members of the U.N. can no longer "be counted on to share our view," and the "majority often opposes the United States on important international questions," so we must "reserve to ourselves the power to determine" how we will act and which matters fall "essentially within the domestic jurisdiction of the United States, as determined by the United States"—in this case, Washington's "unlawful use of force" against Nicaragua.[8]

It is all very well to speak abstractly of the "innovative but justifiable extension of international law" that creates a right of "humanitarian intervention," or to accord to the enlightened states the right to use military force where they "believe it to be just." But it should also be recognized that, hardly by accident, the states that are self-qualified as enlightened turn out to be those that can act as they please. And that in the real world, there are two options:

(1) Some kind of framework of world order, perhaps the U.N. Charter, the International Court of Justice, and other existing institutions, or perhaps something better if it can be devised and broadly accepted.

(2) The powerful do as they wish, expecting to receive the accolades that are the prerogative of power.

Abstract discussion may choose to consider other possible worlds, perhaps a fit topic for graduate seminars in philosophy. But for the present, at least, it is options (1) and (2) that identify the real world in which decisions that affect human affairs have to be made.

The fact that the operative choices reduce to (1) and (2) was recognized fifty years ago by the World Court:[9]

> The Court can only regard the alleged right of intervention as the manifestation of a policy of force, such as has, in the past, given rise to most serious abuses and such as cannot, whatever be the defects in international organization, find a place in international law...; from the nature of things, [intervention] would be reserved for the most powerful states, and might easily lead to perverting the administration of justice itself.

One can adopt the stance of "intentional ignorance" and ignore "custom and practice," or dismiss them on some absurd grounds ("change of course," "Cold War," and other familiar pretexts). Or we can take custom, practice, and explicit doctrine seriously, along with the actual history of "humanitarian intervention," departing from respectable norms but at least opening the possibility of gaining some understanding of what is happening in the world.

Where does that leave the specific question of what should have been done in Kosovo? It leaves it unanswered. The answer cannot be simply deduced from abstract principle, still less from pious hopes, but requires careful attention to the circumstances of the real world.

A reasonable judgment, I think, is that the U.S. chose a course of action that—as anticipated—would escalate atrocities and violence; that strikes yet another blow against the regime of international order, which offers the weak at least some limited protection from predatory states; that undermines democratic developments within Yugoslavia, possibly Macedonia as well; and that sets back the prospects for disarmament and for some control of nuclear weapons and other weapons of mass destruction, indeed may leave others with "no choice" but to "obtain weapons of mass destruction" in self-defense. Of the three logically possible options, it chose (I) "act to escalate the catastrophe," rejecting the alternatives: (II) "do nothing," (III) "try to mitigate the catastrophe." Was option (III) realistic? One cannot know, but there are indications, reviewed earlier, that it might have been.

For Kosovo itself, one plausible observation from the outset was that "every bomb that falls on Serbia and every ethnic killing in Kosovo suggests that it will scarcely be possible for Serbs and Albanians to live beside each other in some sort of peace."[10] Other possible long-term outcomes are not pleasant to contemplate. At best, NATO's immediate institution of its version of the official settlement leaves "staggering problems" to be addressed, most urgently those that are "the effect" of the bombing, as acknowledged.

A standard argument is that we had to do something: we could not simply stand by as atrocities continued. There was no alternative to the resort to force, Tony Blair declared, with many heads nodding in sober agreement: "to do nothing would have been to acquiesce in Milosevic's brutality."[11] If option (III) ("mitigate the catastrophe") is excluded, as tacitly assumed, and we are left only with (I) ("escalate the catastrophe") or (II) ("do nothing"), then we must choose (I). That the argument can even be voiced is a tribute to the desperation of supporters of the bombing. Suppose you see a crime in the streets, and feel that you can't just stand by silently, so you pick up an assault rifle and kill everyone involved: criminal, victim, bystanders. Are we to understand that to be the rational and moral response, in accord with Blair's principle?

One choice, always available, is to follow the Hippocratic principle: "First, do no harm." If you can think of no way to adhere to that elementary principle, then do nothing; at least that is preferable to causing harm—the consequence recognized in advance to be "predictable" in the case of Kosovo, a prediction amply fulfilled. It may sometimes be true that the search for peaceful means is at an end, and that there is "no alternative" to doing nothing or causing vast harm. If so, anyone with even a minimal claim to being a moral agent will abide by the Hippocratic principle. That nothing constructive can be done must, however, be demonstrated. In the case of Kosovo, diplomatic options appeared to be open, and might have been productive, as already discussed, and as is coming to be acknowledged, far too late.

The right of "humanitarian intervention" is likely to be more frequently invoked in coming years—maybe with justification, maybe not—now that the system of deterrence has collapsed (allowing more freedom of action) and Cold War pretexts have lost their efficacy (requiring new ones). In such an era, it may be worthwhile to pay attention to the views of highly respected commentators—not forgetting the World Court, which ruled on the matter of intervention and "humanitarian aid" in a decision rejected by the United States, its essentials not even reported.

In the scholarly disciplines of international affairs and international law it would be hard to find more respected voices than Hedley Bull or Louis Henkin. Bull warned fifteen years ago that "Particular states or groups of states that set themselves up as the authoritative judges of the world common good, in disregard of the views of others, are in fact a menace to international order, and thus to effective action in this field." Henkin, in a standard work on world order, writes that:

[the] pressures eroding the prohibition on the use of force are deplorable, and the arguments to legitimize the use of force in those circumstances are unpersuasive and dangerous...Even "humanitarian intervention" can too readily be used as the occasion or pretext for aggression. Violations of human rights are indeed all too common, and if it were permissible to remedy them by external use of force, there would be no law to forbid the use of force by almost any state against almost any other. Human rights, I believe, will have to be vindicated, and other injustices remedied, by other, peaceful means, not by opening the door to aggression and destroying the principal advance in international law, the outlawing of war and the prohibition of force.[12]

These are reflections that should not be lightly disregarded.

Recognized principles of international law and world order, treaty obligations, decisions by the World Court, considered pronouncements by respected commentators—these do not automatically yield general principles or solutions to particular problems. Each has to be considered on its merits. For those who do not adopt the standards of Saddam Hussein, there is a heavy burden of proof to meet in undertaking the threat or use of force. Perhaps the burden can be met, but that has to be shown, not merely proclaimed. The consequences have to be assessed carefully—in particular, what we take to be "predictable." The reasons for the actions also have to be assessed—on rational grounds, with attention to historical fact and the documentary record, not simply by adulation of our leaders and the "principles and values" attributed to them by admirers.

Notes

Chapter One
"In the Name of Principles and Values"

1. Sources will be identified when we return to the context.
2. The FRY consists of Serbia and Montenegro. NATO and FRY authorities agree on regarding Kosovo as a province of the FRY, part of Serbia with an ambiguous status to which we return. The large Albanian majority long ago made clear its demand for independence. The Albanian term for the region is "Kosova." I will adopt the usage of the U.S. government and other NATO powers, standard international usage as well. Whether that usage is right or wrong, one may debate; the question relates to the basis for the conflict. The term "Kosovars" is often used to refer to Albanian Kosovars. I will keep to the more explicit term "Kosovo Albanians." No term is without misleading connotations.
3. Ann Scales and Louise Palmer, Kevin Cullen, *Boston Globe*, March 25; William Jefferson Clinton, *New York Times*, May 23, 1999. Albright cited in a *Washington Post* retrospective by Barton Gellman, "The Path to Crisis: How the United States and Its Allies Went to War; The Battle for Kosovo, A Defining Atrocity Set Wheels in Motion," *International Herald Tribune*, April 23, 1999.
4. Blair, *Newsweek*, April 19; Roger Cohen, *NYT*, May 16, 1999.
5. University of California Law Professor Michael Glennon, "The New Interventionism," *Foreign Affairs* May/June 1999, lead article.
6. *Ibid*.
7. Thomas Weiss, *Boston Review*, February/March 1994.
8. Friedman, "Foreign Affairs," *NYT*, June 4, 1999.

9. Donald Fox and Michael J. Glennon, "Report to the International Human Rights Law Group and the Washington Office on Latin America," Washington D.C., April 1985, 21. Also Glennon, "Terrorism and 'intentional ignorance'," *Christian Science Monitor*, March 20, 1986. The Report was subjected to intentional ignorance. See my *Necessary Illusions* (South End, 1989), 78.

10. Published by Orwell biographer Bernard Crick in the *Times Literary Supplement*, Sept. 15, 1972; reprinted in Everyman's Library edition. Crick's biography sheds no further light on the matter.

11. Kinzer, *NYT*, June 4, 1999.

12. Editorials, *WP National Weekly Edition*, June 14, 1999.

13. The OSCE consists of most countries of Europe, Turkey, Canada and the U.S.

14. Editorial, *WP Weekly*, March 1, 1986.

15. Amos Gilboa, "NATO is a Danger to the World," *Ma'ariv*, May 9; we return to his broader analysis. Tali Lifkin-Shahak, "Power Won, Peace Lost," *Ma'ariv*, June 10; Solzhenitsyn, AP, April 28; Igor Veksler, TASS, April 27. Draskovic, Steven Erlanger, "A Liberal Threatens Milosevic With Street Protests," *NYT*, April 27, 1999.

16. "Crisis in the World and in the Peace Movement," in Nat Hentoff, ed., *The Essays of A.J. Muste* (Bobbs-Merrill, 1967). See my "Revolutionary Pacifism of A.J. Muste," reprinted in *American Power and the New Mandarins* (Pantheon 1969).

17. Hugh Pope, "Turkey Again Is a Key Strategic Ally of the West," *Wall Street Journal*, May 25, 1999.

18. The phrase is borrowed from the title of one of the first and best of the general studies: Laura Reed and Carl Kaysen, eds., *Emerging Norms of Justified Intervention* (American Academy of Arts and Sciences, 1993).

19. A related argument, commonly voiced, is that the Soviet veto hampered the humanitarian endeavors of the Anglo-Americans, but no longer, with the "wondrous sea change" after "the passing of the cold war" (*NYT* editorial). To sustain the thesis it is necessary to ignore—or often to deny—the fact that since the 1960s, when the U.N. fell out of control, the U.S. has been far in the lead in vetoing Security Council resolutions on a wide range of topics, Britain second, France a distant third. One way to deter understanding is to count all vetoes without differentiating the early ones (mostly Soviet vetoes when power relations guaranteed U.N. obedience to U.S. dictates) from the later ones, as the U.N. came to reflect a broader range of global concerns with

decolonization. On the doctrine and the reality, see *Deterring Democracy* (Verso, 1991; Hill & Wang, 1992), chap. 6.

20. A separate issue is the counterpart: U.S. deterrence of Soviet intervention, which was ugly and brutal but much more limited in scope than that of the West, though inflated in propaganda (including often scholarship) by taking Soviet expansionism to include support for targets of U.S. subversion or aggression. In any event, that component of world disorder is not a prominent feature of the post-Cold War era that sets the time frame for this discussion.

21. Lake, *NYT*, Sept. 26, 1993; *NYT*, Sept. 23, 1994. Steven Holmes, *NYT*, Jan. 3, 1993, cited by Marc Trachtenberg in a review of precedents for the emerging doctrines: "Intervention in Historical Perspective," in Reed and Kaysen, *op. cit.*

22. Sebastian Mallaby, "Uneasy Partners," *NYT Book Review*, Sept. 21, 1997. Senior Administration policymaker cited by Thomas Friedman, *NYT*, Jan. 12, 1992.

23. Glennon, "New Interventionism"; press commentary to which we return.

24. Trachtenberg, *op. cit.*

25. Thomas Fleming, *Independent*, March 7, 1999.

26. Clinton, "A Just and Necessary War."

27. For details on the refugee flows, and the history generally, see Miranda Vickers, *Between Serb and Albanian: A History of Kosovo* (Columbia, 1998).

28. Carlotta Gall, *NYT*, April 5. Summary based on NATO and UNHCR beginning April 1, *NYT*, May 29, 1999, accompanying a John Kifner retrospective. Serbs, Guy Dinmore, *Financial Times*, April 1; Kevin Cullen, *BG*, June 12, 1999. Weller, "The Rambouillet Conference," *International Affairs* 75.2, April 1999. Goss, BBC, "Panorama: War Room, April 19, 1999. UNHCR press release, March 11, 1999.

29. UNHCR figures cited in *BG*, June 5, 1999: 443,100 in Albania, 228,400 in Macedonia. Montenegro and abroad, John Yemma, *BG*, June 6.

30. Yugoslav Red Cross, "Report on the Humanitarian Situation," May 8, 1999.

31. Clinton reports 500 villages destroyed in Kosovo in his victory speech, *NYT*, June 11, 1999. Levi, "Kosovo: It is Here," *Ha'aretz* April 4; Sharon and other Israeli officials, Samdar Peri, *Yediot Ahronot*, April 9; Judy Dempsey, *FT*, April 12. Levi and Sharon cited by Amnon Kapeliouk, *Le Monde diplomatique*, May 1999. Williams, *Middle East*

International, April 23, 1999. See also Peretz Kidron, "Israel: from Kosovo to 'national unity'," *MEI*, April 9; editorial, "Kosovo—1948 revisited," same issue; *Economist*, April 10, 1999. Howe, reporting his shocked discovery in 1982 that the occupation of the territories has had a "coarsening effect" on Israeli society, though not a "corrupting effect," as documented in the book he is reviewing (*NYT Book Review*, May 16, 1982).

32. See my *World Orders Old and New* (Columbia, 1994; extended edition updating U.S.-Israel-Palestine interactions, 1996).

33. On this reconstruction of current history, see my *Fateful Triangle* (South End, 1983, extended 1999); *Pirates and Emperors* (Claremont, 1986; Amana 1988, Black Rose 1988); *World Orders*. Norman Finkelstein, *Image and Reality in the Israel-Palestine Conflict* (Verso, 1995). See *World Orders* (1996, Epilogue), for other recent sources.

34. For extensive discussion, see Chomsky and Edward S. Herman, *Political Economy of Human Rights* (South End, 1979), two volumes; Herman and Chomsky, *Manufacturing Consent* (Pantheon, 1988); Herman, *The Real Terror Network* (South End, 1982); Alexander George, ed., *Western State Terrorism* (Polity, 1991); William Blum, *Killing Hope* (Common Courage, 1995); and many other sources. On the occasional effort to respond, see *Necessary Illusions* and Edward Herman, "The Propaganda Model Revisited," *Monthly Review*, July–August 1998.

35. On the vacillations with regard to Iraq as policy needs shifted, and other similar cases, see *Deterring Democracy* ("Afterword," 1992); *World Orders*; *Powers and Prospects* (South End, 1996). On how Saddam was "pampered and lionized" by Washington and London until he committed the crime of disobedience, see Miron Rezun, *Saddam Hussein's Gulf Wars* (Praeger, 1992), particularly the account of the fawning before the Butcher of Baghdad by a visiting delegation of leading Senators, bringing George Bush's greetings a few months before the invasion of Kuwait. Also Mark Phythian, *Arming Iraq: How the U.S. and Britain Secretly Built Saddam's War Machine* (Northeastern U., 1997); *United States Export Policy Toward Iraq Prior to Iraq's Invasion of Kuwait, Hearing Before the Committee on Banking, Housing, and Urban Affairs*, U.S. Senate, One Hundred Second Congress, Oct. 27, 1992, particularly Gary Milhollin, "Licensing Mass Destruction," pp. 102–20.

36. Hayden, interview with Doug Henwood, WBAI, April 15, 1999. Edited version in Henwood's *Left Business Observer* #89, April 27, 1999.

37. Clark, "Overview," *NYT*, March 27. Also *Sunday Times* (London), March 28: "Nato's supreme commander, Wesley Clark was not surprised at the retaliatory upsurge. 'This was entirely predictable at this stage', he said," referring to the "horrific" impact on civilians. Rubin, "Overview." Clark, *Newsweek*, April 12, 1999.

38. *BG*, April 4, 1999.

39. Elaine Sciolino and Ethan Bronner, *NYT*, April 8, 1999. Goss, *op. cit.* Vickers, *op. cit.*, 273. Press retrospectives confirm Goss's report. The monitors were from the Conference on Security and Cooperation in Europe (CSCE).

40. Jeffrey Smith and William Drozdiak, *WP Weekly*, April 19; John Kifner, *NYT*, May 29, 1999.

41. BBC Summary of World Broadcasts, March 25, 1999, Thursday SECTION: Part 2 Central Europe, the Balkans; FEDERAL REPUBLIC OF YUGOSLAVIA; SERBIA; EE/D3492/A, citing the Tanjug (Yugoslav state) news agency.

42. For recent review on the Middle East, see my *World Orders* and *Fateful Triangle*, and Finkelstein, *op. cit..* On both cases, see *Necessary Illusions*.

Chapter Two
Before the Bombing

1. Jasmina Teodosijevic, "Kosovo: Background," ms., April 1996. For detailed review, see Vickers, *op. cit.*

2. *Ibid.*, 193.

3. *Ibid.*, 235, 239, 213, 228, xif.

4. *Ibid.*, 277; Hooper, "Kosovo: America's Balkan Problem," *Current History*, April 1999. A strong advocate of NATO military action, Hooper is executive director of the Balkan Action Council in Washington, having served in the State Department as deputy director responsible for Balkan affairs, then deputy chief of mission in Warsaw.

5. Vickers, *op. cit.*, 265.

6. Three formal "complaints and requests for investigation and indictment" on the matter have been brought to the Prosecutor of the International Criminal Tribunal on War Crimes in Yugoslavia, including one by a team of Canadian lawyers joined by the American Association of Jurists; Alexander Cockburn, June 21, 1999. I have found no report of any action.

7. Fisk, *Independent* (London), May 15, 1999.

8. William Drozdiak, *WP-BG*, June 9, 1999. On cluster bombs, see below, sec. 3.2, for some illustrations in the '90s.

9. Vickers, Teodosijevic, *op. cit.*

10. Judah, *The Serbs: History, Myth & the Destruction of Yugoslavia* (Yale, 1997).

11. "Just as many Serbs" as Albanians, he writes, which seems dubious given the demography and distribution of power. The more detailed account of population flows given by Vickers leaves the matter obscure.

12. Hedges, "Kosovo's Next Masters," *Foreign Affairs*, May/June 1999.

13. Vickers, *op. cit.*, 268.

14. *op. cit.* See also Hedges, "Victims Not Quite So Innocent," *NYT*, March 28, 1999; Ray Bonner, "NATO Is Wary of Proposals To Help Arm Kosovo Rebels," *NYT*, April 4, 1999.

15. For Judah's current views, see "Inside the KLA," *New York Review*, June 10, 1999.

16. Vickers, *op. cit.*

17. Gellman, *op. cit.* Other accounts report that it was the Interior Ministry police, not the Army, that was the primary agent of repression and target of guerrilla attacks.

18. Judah, *Wall Street Journal*, April 7, 1999.

19. Sciolino and Bronner, *op. cit.*

20. Judah, *op. cit.*, 300f.

21. On the events and reactions/interpretations, see *Fateful Triangle* (1999 edition), 528f., and sources cited; and Human Rights Watch, *Israel/Lebanon: "Operation Grapes of Wrath,"* Sept. 1997. On Peres's mid-1980s "Iron Fist" operations, see *Pirates and Emperors*. On the successful construction of a more useful history, in the U.S. though not in Israel, see these books and also Finkelstein, *op. cit.*, *World Orders* (chap. 3 and "Epilogue").

22. Gellman, *op. cit.*; Smith & Drozdiak, *op. cit.*

23. Evidence is lacking, but it is a natural presumption. See Kifner, *op. cit.*, on the reported increase after the withdrawal of the monitors on March 19. We return to further evidence presented by the U.S. government, but it keeps to 1999.

24. Colum Lynch, *BG*, Oct. 8; Susan Milligan, *BG*, Oct. 9, 1998.

25. Former *Boston Globe* editor Randolph Ryan, who had been working in Yugoslavia for international agencies for several years, and dissident Serb scholar Jasmina Teodosijevic; pc.

26. Justin Brown, "NATO hits Serbia's northern province hard," *CSM*, April 22; Carlotta Gall, "No Water, Power, Phone: A Serbian City's Trials," *NYT*, May 4, 1999.

27. See Canadian historian Floyd Rudmin, *Bordering on Aggression: Evidence of U.S. Military Preparations Against Canada* (Voyageur, 1993).

28. BBC, April 19; see chap. 1, note 41.

29. Frances Williams, international staff, *FT*, Oct. 7, 1998. On the absence of any such authority, see Weller, *op. cit.*, who holds that the bombing was nonetheless justified as "humanitarian intervention," though without argument.

Chapter Three
Assessing Humanitarian Intent

1. For some examples in recent years, see my *Culture of Terrorism* (South End, 1988), chapters 5, 6; *Year 501* (South End, 1993), chap. 7; *Rethinking Camelot* (South End, 1993), chap. 1; only a small sample.

2. See *Deterring Democracy, Year 501, World Orders*, and sources cited, for review. We return to the matter in chap. 6.

3. Cited by Mark Ames and Matt Taibbi, *Counterpunch*, May 16–30.

4. There has been some controversy, based primarily on accounts by mainstream French reporters. See *Covert Action Quarterly*, Spring-Summer 1999, for review. What matters here is the perception, not the facts.

5. Americas Watch (now Human Rights Watch/Americas), *A Year of Reckoning* (March 1990). Ames and Taibbi, *op. cit.*

6. Koppel, *Nightline*, ABC-TV, Jan. 29; Jeffrey Smith, "This Time, Walker Wasn't Speechless; Memory of El Salvador Spurred Criticism of Serbs," *WP*, Jan. 23, 1999. Cited by Mark Cook, *CAQ*, Spring-Summer 1999.

7. Not entirely. Thus the *Economist* now cites a figure of 250,000 people killed by "massacres and famine," "nearly a third of the present population," while "appalling intimidation and torture have been commonplace" (May 1, 1999). But in giving these (probably exaggerated) figures, it fails to recall its own stand long after the facts were well known: that the great mass murderer and torturer who extended his achievements beyond Indonesia itself with his invasion of the neighboring territory is "at heart benign," and that the tales of atrocities are concocted by "propagandists for the guerrillas" with their "talk of the army's savagery and use of torture" (Aug. 15, 1987). On East Timor

(and the elite reaction), see *Political Economy of Human Rights*, vol. I, and my *Towards a New Cold War* (Pantheon, 1982). On more recent events and coverage, see among others *Powers and Prospects* and sources cited.

8. Mark Dodd, *Age* (Australia), May 1, April 30, 1999. John Aglionby, *Observer* (London), April 25, 1999, reporting on Suai and also, from the scene, on the reign of terror in the coffee-growing center of Ermera. Lindsay Murdoch and Peter Cole-Adams, "Freedom Slaughtered," *Sydney Morning Herald*, April 19. Aid workers, Tim Dodd and Greg Earl, *Australian Financial Review*, Feb. 27–28. Murdoch, *Age*, May 6 (with Brendan Nicholson), 7, 8. Murphy interviewed by Murdoch, *Age*, March 10. Dodd, "Outspoken US doctor forced out," *Sydney Morning Herald*, May 17, 1999. Lindsay Murdoch, "Wall of military blocks doctors," *Sydney Morning Herald*, June 3, 1999. On Liquica and other massacres, also *TAPOL Bulletin* No. 152, May 1999, London.

9. Brian Woodley, *Australian*, May 14. Peter Hartcher, *Australian Financial Review*, May 1, 1999, citing former Australian military officer Bob Lowry, "the man who wrote the book on the subject" of ABRI.

10. McNaughtan, *Sydney Morning Herald*, April 20; Mark Riley, *Sydney Morning Herald*, April 22; Murdoch and Nicholson, *Age*, May 6, 1999.

11. Fran Abrams, "What Cook said, What is happening," *Independent*, May 23; World in Action, June 2, 1997. Richard Norton-Taylor and Lucy Ward, "Ministers attacked over military export licences," *Guardian*, May 15; Fran Abrams, "Britain still selling Indonesia arms," *Independent*, May 15; Michael Evans, "Britain accused of selling Jakarta anti-riot weapons," *Times*, May 15, 1998. Michael Prescott and Zoe Brennan, "Cook sells twice as many guns to Indonesia as Tories," *Sunday Times*, March 14; Pilger, "Blood on British Hands," *Guardian*, Jan. 25, 1999. O'Shaughnessy, "Arms and aid to Indonesia—it's business as usual," *Independent on Sunday*, July 13, 1997. Reuters, "US bans use of its weapons in Timor," *Age*, Oct. 23, 1998. Clinton evasions: Reuters, *NYT*, Dec. 8, 1993, a few lines on an inside page; Irene Wu, *Far Eastern Economic Review*, June 30, 1994. See *Powers and Prospects*, chap. 8, for further detail.

12. Haq, IPS, May 28, 1998.

13. *Ibid*.

14. Mark Dodd, "Military caught in the act," *Age*, May 21, 1999.

15. Mark Dodd, *Sunday Age*, May 23, 1999.

16. *Nation*, Feb. 16, 1980, reviewing *Political Economy of Human Rights*, which elicited huge outrage by comparing East Timor to Cambodia in

the same years. A standard reaction has been that comparison of East Timor to Cambodia constitutes apologetics for Pol Pot. Apart from the transparent falsehood, it is evident that the reaction does in fact express shameful apologetics—for the U.S.-backed Indonesian crimes; evident, but unintelligible to articulate opinion across a broad spectrum, facts that offer a revealing insight into the effectiveness of indoctrination in free societies.

17. U.S. State Department, "Colombia Country Report on Human Rights Practices for 1998."

18. Among others, Human Rights Watch, *Colombia's Killer Networks: The Military-Paramilitary Partnership and the United States* (New York, 1996); *War without Quarter* (October 1998). On the background, see *World Orders* and sources cited; Javier Giraldo S.J., *Colombia: The Genocidal Democracy* (Common Courage, 1996). For more recent update, see NACLA *Report on the Americas*, March/April 1998, and the regular publications of the Colombia Support Network and other human rights and solidarity groups.

19. I was one of the AI delegation members.

20. *Colombia's Killer Networks*, citing Michael McClintock's very important study *Instruments of Statecraft* (Pantheon, 1992).

21. See *World Orders* and sources cited, particularly AI, HRW, and the Washington Office on Latin America (WOLA). *Colombia Bulletin*, Spring 1999, citing many press sources. One particularly well-researched case, investigated by an OAS commission, involved hideous chain-saw massacres and other torture. See *Comisión de Investigación de los sucesos violentos de Trujillo: Informe Final* (Colombia, Jan. 1995). President Gavíria brushed aside requests for inquiry for four years, but to his credit, his successor Ernesto Samper accepted the report, apparently a historic first: the commanding officer responsible, who had been rewarded by promotion, was punished by removal from active service, a harsher punishment than most.

22. Note that Israel was not under attack by a superpower—or, in fact, under severe military threat apart from the latter weeks of May 1948, when Arab armies entered the conflict, which took place almost entirely in the designated Palestinian state, eventually partitioned between Israel and (British-dominated) Jordan. By May about 300,000 refugees had already fled in the course of civil conflict. By the end of May, after receipt of Czech arms, Israel's military superiority was never in serious doubt, facts now recognized in serious histories. See, among

others, Israeli historian Ilan Pappé, *The Making of the Arab-Israeli Conflict 1947–1951* (I.B. Tauris, 1992).

23. See chap. 1, note 4.

24. Kurdish Human Rights Project (KHRP, London), *1998 Annual Report*, April 1999, reviewing Court judgments during 1998.

25. David Buchan, *FT*, "Balkan conflict brings its own harsh dilemmas," June 15, 1999; the "dilemmas" have to do in part with "parallels" between Kosovo and the "Kurdish problem" of Turkey, "loyal as ever to Nato" as it bombed Serbia.

26. See Jonathan Randal, *After Such Knowledge, What Forgiveness: My Encounters with Kurdistan* (Westview 1999); John Tirman, *Spoils of War: The Human Cost of America's Arms Trade* (Free Press, 1997). For background, see David McDowall, *A Modern History of the Kurds* (I.B. Tauris-St. Martin's, 1997); Michael Gunter, *The Kurds and the Future of Turkey* (St. Martin's, 1997); Robert Olson, ed. *The Kurdish National Movement in the 1990s* (Kentucky, 1996). On the atrocities of the '90s, see particularly Human Rights Watch, *Forced Displacement of Ethnic Kurds from Southeastern Turkey* (Oct. 1994) and *Weapons Transfers and Violations of the Laws of War in Turkey* (Nov. 1995); David McDowall, *The Destruction of Villages in South-East Turkey* (Medico International and KHRP, June 1996); Tirman, *Spoils of War* on "Turkey's 'White Genocide'" and the crucial U.S. role in implementing it. For current coverage, see Kevin McKiernan, "Turkey's War on the Kurds," *Bulletin of the Atomic Scientists*, March/April 1999; Tamar Gabelnick, Acting Director of the Arms Sales Monitoring Project of the Federation of American Scientists, "Turkey: Arms and Human Rights," *Foreign Policy In Focus* 4.16, May 1999 (Interhemispheric Resource Center). Also Nicole Pope, "Turkey's Missed Chance," *NYT* Op-ed, April 17, 1999, a welcome break from the normal pattern.

27. See Ismail Besikci, *Selected Writings: Kurdistan and Turkish Colonialism* (Kurdish Solidarity Committee, London, Dec. 1991), including a formal protest by leading British writers, scholars, and parliamentarians. Besikci had refused a $10,000 prize by the U.S. Fund for Free Expression in protest against U.S. government support for Turkish repression.

28. Tirman, *op. cit.*; on the village guards, see Human Rights Watch reports cited.

29. See McClintock, *op. cit.*, for extensive detail; Blum, *op. cit.*, for recent review.

30. Randal, *op. cit.*; KHRP and Bar Human Rights Committee of England and Wales, *Policing Human Rights Abuses in Turkey*, May 1999.

31. *Ibid.* The Minister was sacked.

32. Randal, Human Rights Watch, Tirman, McKiernan, *op. cit.*

33. Since such methods of wholesale terror are the prerogatives of the more powerful, they are considered less atrocious or insignificant, perhaps even meritorious. Thus My Lai was considered a horrifying atrocity, but not planned slaughter of civilians and huge ethnic cleansing operations conducted by carpet bombing of densely populated areas. For comparison of the My Lai massacre and the military operation to which it was a footnote, see the detailed inquiry by *Newsweek* Saigon Bureau chief Kevin Buckley and his associates reviewed in *Political Economy of Human Rights*, vol. I.

34. *Policing Human Rights Abuses.*

35. Gabelnick, *op. cit.*

36. Leyla Boulton, *FT*, April 8, 1999. Reuters, "Turkish F-16s said to carry out bomb raids," *BG*, May 18, reporting "sharply increasing" strikes from Turkish bases and laudable "humanitarian efforts" as Turkey admits thousands of Albanian refugees.

37. Gabelnick, *op. cit.* On the vicissitudes of the Kurds as "worthy/unworthy victims," see Randal, *op. cit.* Also *Necessary Illusions*, App. 5.2.

38. Lawyers Committee for Human Rights, *Critique: Review of the U.S. Department of State's Country Reports on Human Rights Practices for 1994*, Middle East and North Africa section (New York, 1995), 255.

39. Tirman, *op. cit.* Gore quoted by Carol Midgalovitz, "Turkey's Kurdish Imbroglio and U.S. Policy" (Congressional Research Service, 1994), cited by Vera Saeedpour, *Covert Action Quarterly*, Fall 1995.

40. On the treatment of Ocalan's lawyers, see KHRP, Bar Human Rights Committee of England and Wales, and Howe & Co. Solicitors, *Intimidation in Turkey*, May 1999. One lawyer has himself been jailed repeatedly, also tortured, for such crimes as using the words "Kurdish" and "Kurdistan" and translating a Kurdish talk for the Human Rights Association of Turkey.

41. Kinzer, *NYT*, May 31, June 1; "Kurd's Rebel Leader May Prove a Discredit to His Cause," Feb. 17, 1999.

42. AP, *BG*, June 10, 1999. See Chap. 1, notes 11, 12.

43. "Kosovo and Beyond," *New York Review*, June 24, 1999, published several weeks earlier; article dated May 27. The comparison is commonly taken to be an obvious truth. Thus, Moscow correspondent Michael

Wines, describing the sorry state of Russian culture, shakes his head sadly at the spectacle of Russian war veterans on the anniversary of the "Allied victory over the Nazis" (overwhelmingly, the Russian victory over the Nazis): "None of them saw any parallel between Hitler's massacre of six million Jews and the killings or expulsions of Kosovo Albanians. Nor did any draw a distinction between the NATO alliance and the United States," revealing both their moral degeneracy and their ignorance of world affairs. "World War II Veterans Now Angry at an Old Ally," *NYT*, May 10, 1999.

44. The reaction to mass slaughter in Indonesia in 1965 is perhaps the most startling recent example. See *Year 501*, chap. 4, for review; see chap. 6, below.

45. Christopher de Bellaigne, *NYR*, June 24, 1999, reviewing Henri Barkey and Graham Fuller, *Turkey's Kurdish Question* (Rowman & Littlefield, 1998).

46. See particularly Randal, *op. cit.*; also references of note 27.

47. George Robertson, *Freedom, the Individual and the Law* (Penguin, 7th edition, 1993), a standard source on civil liberties in Britain. Churchill, see my *Turning the Tide* (South End, 1985); on both Churchill and Lloyd George, see *World Orders*; and sources cited. Wilbur Edel, "Diplomatic History—State Department Style," *Political Science Quarterly* 106.4, 1991–92. The secrecy project expanded under Clinton, leading to warnings by the State Department historians' committee that the official historical record may become "an official lie"; Tim Weiner, *NYT,* April 9, 1998. Concealment and destruction of CIA files on the 1953–54 coups in Iran and Guatemala is an egregious example. On the significance of this "obituary for the openness program" with most of the evidence destroyed, see the 1999 introduction by Nick Cullather to his 1993 internal CIA study, *Secret History* (Indiana, 1999). On the sanitizing of the official record concerning the enormous U.S. clandestine operation to break up Indonesia and take over its primary resources in 1958, see Audrey and George Kahin, *Subversion as Foreign Policy* (New Press, 1995).

48. See MAG (Mines Advisory Group) (Manchester U.K., nd). Co-laureate of the 1997 Nobel Peace Prize, MAG is a U.K. charitable organization funded by church groups, the European Union, UNICEF, and the British Government. It has been devoted to publicity and action related to landmines and anti-personnel weapons generally, working on the ground in Afghanistan, Southeast Asia, Africa, and the Middle East.

49. Wain, "The Deadly Legacy of War in Laos," *Asia Wall Street Journal*, Jan. 24, 1997. Padraic Convery, "Living a footstep away from death," *Guardian Weekly*, Oct. 4, 1998. Marcus Warren, "America's undeclared war still killing children," *Sunday Telegraph*, April 20, 1997. Ronald Podlaski, Veng Saysana and James Forsyth, *Accidental Massacre: American Air-Dropped Bomblets Have Continued to Maim and Slaughter Thousands of Innocent Victims, Mostly Children, for the Last 23 Years in Indochina* (Humanitarian Liaison Services, Warren Vermont, 1997); Podlaski served in Vietnam in secret cross-border operations and moved to Cambodia to establish a prosthetics center in 1991, Forsyth is a British businessman and former reporter who has worked in Asia and the U.S; both have been working in Laos, and both believe that the official figures of 20,000 people blown up every year, over half killed, are too low (Wain, *op. cit.*). Mennonite Central Committee Bombie Removal Project, *A Deadly Harvest*, nd. Fred Branfman, "Something Missing: A Visit to the Plain of Jars," *Indochina Newsletter* (Cambridge MA) no. 4, 1995. A Lao-speaking IVS volunteer, Branfman did far more than anyone to try to expose the crimes in the Plain of Jars from the 1960s; see his *Voices from the Plain of Jars* (Harper & Row, 1972). See also my *At War with Asia* (Pantheon, 1970), *For Reasons of State* (Pantheon, 1973). Also *Political Economy of Human Rights* vol. II, and sources cited, and on coverage, *Manufacturing Consent*.

50. MAG, see preceding note. Keith Graves, "US secrecy puts bomb disposal team in danger," *Sunday Telegraph*, Jan. 4, 1998. Matthew Chance, "Secret war still claims lives in Laos," *Independent*, June 27, 1997. Matthew Pennington, "Inside Indochina," *Bangkok Post*, Feb. 20, 1996, citing reports of the Cambodian Mines Action Center; Pascale Trouillaud, AFP, *Bangkok Post*, May 14, 1996.

51. Daniel Pruzin, "US Clears Laos of the Unexploded," *CSM* Sept. 9, 1996. Cameron Barr, "One Man's Crusade to Destroy Bombs," *CSM*, April 29, 1997.

52. Paul Watson, *Los Angeles Times*, April 28, 1999.

53. Killing Secrets Campaign, *Kosovo: "A Wasteland Called Peace,"* May 1999, Cumbria U.K.

54. *FT*, June 4; Kosovo Peace Accord, *NYT*, June 4, 1999.

55. Kevin Cullen and Anne Kornblut, *BG*, April 4; Clinton Speech of April 1 at Norfolk Air Station, *NYT*, April 2, 1999.

56. Lynch, "US seen leaving Africa to solve its own crises," *BG*, Feb. 19, 1999. Lynch reports that Clinton refused "less than $100,000" for the Congo operation.

57. Paul Starr, "The Choice in Kosovo," *American Prospect*. July–August 1999. The citation is unfair; the reaction is close to uniform.

58. See chap. 1, note 4.

59. Halliday, "Iraq and the UN's Weapon of Mass Destruction," *Current History*, Feb. 1999.

60. John Mueller and Karl Mueller, "Sanctions of Mass Destruction," *Foreign Affairs* May/June 1999. Shorrock, *Guardian Weekly*, May 2, 1999.

61. From the declassified record. For more extensive quotes, and discussion of measures to increase the punishment after the end of the Cold War enlarged the range of opportunities, see my *Profit Over People* (Seven Stories, 1998), chap. 3.

62. Columbia University professor of preventive diplomacy David Phillips, cited by Ethan Bronner, "The Scholars: Historians Note Flaws in President's Speech," *NYT*, March 26, 1999.

63. See Stephen Shalom, "Gravy Train: Feeding the Pentagon by Feeding Somalia," *Z magazine*, Feb. 1993;, Alex de Waal, "Humanitarian War Crimes," *New Left Review* 230, July/August 1998. See also Alex de Waal and Rakiya Omaar, "Doing Harm by Doing Good? The International Relief Effort in Somalia," *Current History*, May 1993; African Rights (London), *Somalia Operation Restore Hope: A Preliminary Assessment*, May 1993, and *Somalia: Human Rights Abuses by the United Nations Forces*, July 1993. On press coverage, see my "'Mandate for Change,' or business as usual," *Z magazine*, Feb. 1993.

64. Richard Dowden, *Independent*, Dec. 13, 1998; *Observer*, March 22 1998; *Guardian Weekly*, March 29 1998 (referring to a recently published book by U.S. journalist Mark Bowden who covered the events, *Black Hawk Down*). Eric Schmitt, *NYT*, Dec. 8, 1993. See also De Waal, *op. cit.*

65. John Balzar, "Marines firing as UN leaves Somalia," *BG-LAT*, March 4, 1995. Maynes, *FP*, Spring 1995. Steven Lee Myers, "A Marine General Who Studies Cultures as Well as Bomb Targets in the Gulf," *NYT*, Dec. 27, 1998.

66. De Waal, *op. cit.*

67. Karl Vick, "Somalia Stares Starvation in the Face Again," *WP Weekly*, Jan. 4, 1999. An extract from Mark Bowden's *Black Hawk Down* was presented as a page-long editorial in the *Boston Globe* (May 31, 1999),

keeping to the suffering of U.S. troops. There was no explanation, but it was presumably meant as a warning about dispatch of U.S. troops to the Balkans.

68. For background, see *Year 501* and sources cited. For more recent review and sources, see *Profit Over People*, chap. 4.

69. Lisa McGowan, *Democracy Undermined, Economic Justice Denied: Structural Adjustment and the AID Juggernaut in Haiti* (Washington: Development Gap, Jan. 1997). Jennifer Bauduy, "US Chickens Steal Jobs From—Haiti?," *CSM*, Sept. 15, 1998.

70. Talbott testimony before a Senate Committee on the impending withdrawal in mid-1995, cited by Morris Morley and Chris McGillion, "'Disobedient' Generals and the Politics of Redemocratization: The Clinton Administration and Haiti," *Political Science Quarterly* 112.3, 1997.

71. See my "United States and the 'Challenge of Relativity'," in Tony Evans, ed., *Human Rights Fifty Years On: A Reappraisal* (Manchester University Press/St. Martin's Press, 1998); Detlev Vagts, "Taking Treaties Less Seriously," "Editorial Comments," *AJIL* 92:458 (1998).

72. William Glaberson, *NYT*, March 27.

73. See Amnesty International, *The United States of America: Rights for All*, 1998.

74. Murphy, *Humanitarian Intervention: The United Nations in an Evolving World Order* (Pennsylvania, 1996). Citations are from his 1994 doctoral dissertation with the same title. For review, see *American Journal of International Law*, vol 92, 1998, 583f. On Japan's actions and rhetoric in Manchuria, as compared with those of the U.S. in Vietnam, see "Revolutionary Pacifism of A.J. Muste," reprinted in *American Power and the New Mandarins*.

75. For a judicious review, focusing on Kissinger's behavior and subsequent self-justification, see Raymond Garthoff, *Détente and Confrontation* (Brookings Institution, 1985). Kissinger virtually concedes the point in his evasive apologia, *White House Years*, p. 854. On this generally outlandish memoir, see *Towards a New Cold War*.

76. Gaddis, "The Old World Order," *NYT Sunday Book Review*, March 21, 1999.

77. On the events and TR's interpretation of them, see David Stannard, *American Holocaust* (Oxford, 1992).

78. Thomas Bailey. *A Diplomatic History of the American People* (Appleton-Century-Crofts, 1969).

79. Ernest May and Philip Zelikow, *The Kennedy Tapes* (Harvard, 1997). For a very illuminating review of the events and interpretation, see Louis Pérez, *The War of 1898* (U. of North Carolina, 1998), the source of quotes below.

80. Not entirely. Mark Twain was a notable exception, though his bitter condemnations of the savagery of the invaders suffered the usual fate of "unpopular ideas." See Jim Zwick, ed. *Mark Twain's Weapons of Satire: Anti-Imperialist Writings on the Philippine-American War* (Syracuse, 1992); for a small sample of his trenchant observations, see *Year 501*.

81. On the Concert of Europe and other precedents, see Trachtenberg, *op. cit.*

82. Clive Ponting, *Churchill* (Sinclair-Stevenson, 1994), 132.

83. Glennon, "The New Interventionism."

84. *Ibid.*

85. On the interesting concept of "anti-Americanism," a concept with counterparts primarily (perhaps only) in totalitarian states and military dictatorships, see my *Letters from Lexington: Reflections on Propaganda* (Common Courage, 1993), chap. 17.

86. See Roger Owen, *The Middle East in the World Economy: 1800–1914* (London, New York, 1981); Leila Tarazi Fawaz, *Occasion for War* (University of California, 1994). I am indebted to Irene Gendzier and Elaine Hagopian for information and sources.

Chapter Four
The Denial Syndrome

1. Gellman, *op. cit.*

2. John Broder, *NYT*, June 3, 1999, reporting Clinton's address at the Air Force Academy graduation. Correctly but irrelevantly, Clinton adds that assaults on the Albanian Kosovars had been planned for months, probably for years.

3. Serge Schmemann, "From President, Victory Speech And a Warning," *NYT*, June 11, 1999.

4. Adam Clymer, *NYT*, March 29; Clinton Speech, *NYT*, April 2; Bacon, Bob Hohler, *BG*, April 3; Jane Perlez, *NYT*, March 28, 1999, and many others.

5. Glennon, Smith and Drozdiak, *op. cit.*; editorial, *WSJ*, April 16, 1999.

6. *NYT*, April 18, 1999. AI, *United States of America, op. cit.* Human Rights Watch, *Shielded from Justice* (June 1998). On the U.S. and the

UD, see my "United States and the 'Challenge of Relativity'," and sources cited. On human rights violations abroad, the literature is voluminous, a small sample already cited. One relevant finding, difficult to ignore on rational grounds (though easily set aside on doctrinal grounds), is the correlation between foreign aid and torture in Latin America, including military aid and running through the Carter years, revealed by the pre-eminent scholar in this area, Lars Schoultz: *Comparative Politics*, Jan. 1981. For the Reagan years, the correlation was too obvious to study, and Colombia alone illustrates its persistence to the present. Also a more comprehensive study by economist Edward Herman, extending beyond the Western Hemisphere and bringing in factors that account for the correlation on reasonable grounds as a secondary effect of the expected correlation of foreign aid with improvement of the investment climate; *Real Terror Network*, also reviewed in *Political Economy of Human Rights*, vol. I.

7. U.S. Department of State, "Erasing History: Ethnic Cleansing in Kosovo," State Department website, http://www.state.gov/-index.html, May 1999.

8. See chap. 1, note 41.

9. Weller, *op. cit.*; see chap. 1, note 29.

10. Roger Cohen, *NYT*, May 28, 1999. Accompanying front-page story by Jane Perlez. Two full pages are devoted to a summary of "key sections."

11. Philip Shenon, *NYT*, May 27, 1999.

12. It could be argued that the effort to prevent such events motivated the prior undertaking, but inspection of the cases rules this out very clearly.

13. Paul Wilson, introducing Havel's address to the Canadian Parliament: "Kosovo and the End of the Nation-State," *New York Review*, June 10, 1999.

14. Excerpts, *NYT*, Feb. 22; *WP Weekly*, March 5, 1990. *WP*, see chap. 1, note 14.

15. For more on this instructive episode and others that accompanied it, see *Deterring Democracy*, chap. 10.

16. Lewis, "Which Side Are We On," *NYT*, May 29, 1999.

17. David Rohde, "Wiesel, a Man of Peace, Cites Need to Act," *NYT*, June 2, 1999.

18. Yoav Karni, "The Prophet from New York," *Ha'aretz*, June 27, 1985. See *Turning the Tide* for further comment, and *Fateful Triangle* for additional examples of Wiesel's principle of maintaining silence in the face of atrocities. The fellow Laureate was MIT biologist Salvador Luria,

who had asked me to collect documentation from the Hebrew press for
him to send to Wiesel along with his (unanswered) suggestion.

19. Bauer, Israel Amrani, *Ha'aretz*, April 20, 1990. The context of the article was the decision of state television to cancel a documentary on the
Armenian genocide under pressure from the government, and allegedly
from immigrants from Turkey who feared that "the broadcast would
harm Israel-Turkey relations." See Israel Charny, "The Conference
Crisis: The Turks, Armenians and the Jews," in *International Conference
on the Holocaust and Genocide*, Tel Aviv, June 20–24, 1982, Book One
(Tel Aviv, 1983) (cited by Peter Novick, *The Holocaust in American
Life*, Houghton Mifflin, 1999). Wiesel has been sharply condemned in
the Israeli press for his subordination to state power and his principle
of silence in the face of atrocities. For a sample of reports from the
mainstream press when he was awarded the Nobel Peace Prize, see
Alexander Cockburn, *Nation*, Nov. 8, 1986.

20. David Shribman, "An oft-battered Clinton emerges victorious again,"
BG, June 11, 1999.

21. 1999 Federal Information Systems Corporation, Federal News Service,
April 1, 1999.

22. Kai Bird, *Nation*, June 14, 1999.

23. Roger Cohen, *NYT*, March 30, 1999, quoting a State Department official.

24. Eric Schmitt and Steven Lee Myers, "NATO Said to Focus Raids on
Serb Elite's Property," *NYT*, April 19; Guy Dinmore, "'Tomahawk
democracy' decried as car plant bombed," *FT*, April 10/11, 1999. On
the labor movement, see Elaine Bernard, head of Harvard's Trade
Union Program, "Independent Unions in Yugoslavia," webpost (Znet,
www.zmag.org), April 4, 1999.

25. The program targeted "the economic infrastructure" generally. The
goal was to bring "economic life nearly to a standstill" from Vojvodina
in the North to the rest of Yugoslavia, reducing it to a level that made
"prospects for economic reconstruction seem bleak" with "permanent
damage" to electricity and water supplies from high-explosive bombs.
Water supply in Belgrade was reduced by 90%, hospitals "having the
most trouble." Michael Dobbs, "Bombing devastates Serbia's infrastructure," *WP-BG*, April 29; Steven Erlanger, "Production Cut in Half,
Experts Say," *NYT*, April 30; Erlanger, "Reduced to a 'Caveman' Life,"
NYT, May 19, 1999; and many other reports from the scene.

26. Pfaff, *BG*, May 31, 1999.

27. Pfaff, *Condemned to Freedom* (Random House, 1971). See *For Reasons of State* for these and many similar reflections. As noted there, Pfaff is closely paraphrasing comments by Townsend Hoopes in a book that appeared two years earlier, though without citation; but since Hoopes mentions Pfaff it is unclear who deserves the credit.

28. April 19, 1999.

29. See chap. 3, note 43.

30. For a review of coverage, more accurately non-coverage, see *Manufacturing Consent*. On Kennedy's war, see *Rethinking Camelot*, and on the final paroxysm of U.S. violence in its war against South Vietnam, *Political Economy of Human Rights*, vol. I, relying in part on extensive unpublished studies by Kevin Buckley, *Newsweek* Saigon Bureau chief, provided to us. Some of the most revealing records of U.S. atrocities, and the reasons for them, are in the detailed studies by U.S. advisors; see *Rethinking Camelot* for some illustrations.

31. Among others, Stacy Sullivan, "Milosevic's Willing Executioners," *New Republic*, May 10, 1999. Goldhagen's original thesis on "Hitler's Willing Executioners" has achieved much popular renown but has not fared very brilliantly in the scholarly literature; similarly the application to Serbia. For a detailed critical analysis of the original, see Norman Finkelstein and Ruth Bettina Birn, *A Nation on Trial* (Holt 1998). On the application to Serbia see Charles King, *Times Literary Supplement*, May 7, 1999.

32. Editorials, *NR*, May 2, 1981; April 2, 1984.

33. Editor Martin Peretz, "Lebanon Eyewitness," *NR*, Aug. 2, 1982. For more on this and similar contributions at the time, see *Fateful Triangle*.

34. *NYT*, May 9, 1999.

35. *NYT*, April 23, 1999.

36. See chap. 3, note 78.

37. I know of one example: "Apaches and Tomahawks," *Le Monde diplomatique*, May 1999.

38. On the Seminole wars, see William Earl Weeks, *John Quincy Adams and American Global Empire* (Kentucky, 1992).

39. Tirman, *op. cit..* On the celebration in children's texts, see *At War with Asia*. On the massacre, *Year 501* and sources cited.

40. Weeks, *op. cit.*; see *Rethinking Camelot*, introduction, for further sources and discussion of contemporary relevance.

41. On the attribution of "good intentions" in initiating and sustaining decades of unusual horror in Guatemala, see Piero Gleijeses, "The

Culture of Fear," Afterword to Cullather, *op. cit.* The record on Indochina is particularly astonishing. One revealing example is the reaction to Robert McNamara's shameful apologetics, denounced as treachery by the right, hailed as vindication by prominent opponents of the Vietnam war. See my "Hamlet without the Prince," *Diplomatic History* 20.3, Summer 1996; and more generally, "Memories," Z, Summer 1995.

42. Shribman, *op. cit.*

43. Peter Berkowitz, Professor of government at Harvard and author of *Virtue and the Making of Modern Liberalism*, "Liberalism and Kosovo. The Good Fight," *New Republic*, May 10, 1999.

44. Kissinger, "Commentary," BG, March 1, 1999. *American Foreign Policy* (Norton, 1969).

45. Tony Judt, "Tyrannized by Weaklings," Op-ed, *NYT*, April 5; Serge Schmemann, "A New Collision of East and West," *NYT*, April 4, 1999. Ash, *op. cit.*

46. Michael Wines, *NYT*, June 13, 1999.

47. On the Kishinev and Sabra/Shatila massacres (a comparison brought up in the Israeli press) and other gruesome crimes at about the same time that passed unnoticed, see *Fateful Triangle*.

48. Wines, note 45.

49. Robert Marquand, *NYT*, CSM, June 14, 1999, quoting Blair and Havel. He properly singles out "the most aggrieved minority, the Kurds of Turkey and neighboring countries," unfortunately "sidelined in the wake of the capture and trial" of Ocalan. Quite the contrary, the capture and shockingly fraudulent trial of Ocalan for a moment broke the approved silence on the "grievances" of the Kurds of Turkey, though the U.S. role remained properly concealed. There was no way to "sideline" an issue that had never even made the playing field, and were the West really to take seriously the principles and values it formally espouses, the capture of Ocalan would have intensified the already huge protest over its shameful role.

Chapter Five
The Diplomatic Record

1. Roger Cohen, May 27; Susan Milligan and Kevin Cullen, BG, May 27; Susan Milligan, BG, May 28; Erlanger, NYT, May 27; Milligan, "NATO launches heaviest raids," BG, May 28, 1999.

2. *WP*, May 27, 1999.

3. Jane Perlez, *NYT*, Feb. 11, 1999. Former Bush administration National Security Council official Richard Haas of the Brookings Institute, quoted by Jonathan Landay, "How a NATO strike on Serbs could set precedent," *CSM*, Jan. 21, 1999.

4. Kevin Cullen, "U.S., Europeans in Discord over Kosovo," *BG*, Feb. 22, 1999.

5. See Weller, *op. cit.*, a detailed review by a knowledgeable participant who was Legal Advisor to the Kosova (Kosovo Albanian) delegation that was headed at Rambouillet by KLA leader Hashim Thaci.

6. *Interim Agreement for Peace and Self-Government in Kosovo*, privately circulated, from the internet.

7. There is one qualification: the Chief of the Implementation Mission of the OSCE "is the final authority" regarding his functions concerning supervision of withdrawal of Yugoslav forces and police.

8. Steven Erlanger, *NYT*, June 5, quoting the wording of the article; Blaine Harden, *NYT*, same day, oblique reference. Dinmore, "Belgrade may still secure better deal," *FT*, June 6, 1999.

9. Editorial, *BG*, June 18, 1999. The editors initially joined in support for the bombing, then came to question it on tactical grounds, and finally saw it as a victory for Clinton, conceding their error.

10. AFP, March 23; Inter Press Service, March 23; Deutsche Presse-Agentur, March 23; TASS, March 23. It was not reported by UPI (George Nash) or AP (Robert Reid) March 23, though there is a March 24 AP report by Dusan Stojanovic from Belgrade. One exception to the general silence was the *Detroit Free Press*, which gave the essence of the wire service reports. The BBC reported the main text (see chap. 1, note 41), but apparently not the reference to an "international presence" reported by the wire services. The first mention I found in the mainstream U.S. press is by Steven Erlanger, reporting from Belgrade (*NYT*, April 8), though the Resolution does not go quite as far as he indicates in a late paragraph.

11. FAIR Action Alert: "Was a Peaceful Kosovo Solution Rejected by U.S.?," April 14, 1999.

12. Craig Whitney, *NYT*, April 11, 1999. A regular refrain, David Peterson notes (pc), citing also Whitney's articles on March 26, April 7, June 6, with virtually the same wording.

13. The only U.S. newspaper to break ranks was *Newsday*, which covered developments fully and accurately. It is perhaps surprising that high-level leaks should go to a suburban New York newspaper rather than to

the *New York Times*, though the fact that *Newsday* is found—in this case with blaring headlines—on every New York City newsstand does suggest a reason for the choice. For regular review as the process was proceeding, see my articles in Z magazine. See *Deterring Democracy* (chap. 6 and "Afterword") and my article in Cynthia Peters, ed., *Collateral Damage* (South End, 1992), for extensive review; also Douglas Kellner, *The Persian Gulf TV War* (Westview, 1992). The matter is reviewed in the best of the general histories: Dilip Hiro, *Desert Shield to Desert Storm* (HarperCollins, 1992). It is ignored in others, including the highly-regarded study by Lawrence Freedman and Efraim Karsh, *The Gulf Conflict 1990–1991: Diplomacy and War in the New World Order* (Princeton, 1992), which praises "the scope and originality of our analysis," using "evidence from *all* available sources," contrasting their achievement with mere journalism—and in fact ignoring all crucial documentary and other sources, along with other oversights and errors in a rather unpleasant form of apologetics. For details, see my "World Order and its Rules: Variations on Some Themes," *J. of Law and Society* (Cardiff Law School), Summer 1993.

14. Steven Erlanger, *NYT*, April 23; Bob Hohler, *BG*, April 23, 1999; Chronology, *WSJ*, June 4.

15. Steven Erlanger, *NYT*, May 1, 1999. Erlanger, who evidently was aware of the facts, reiterates within the story that "even before the bombing, the Serb legislature had approved the idea of a United Nations presence in Kosovo." See note 10.

16. Interview, *NYT*, May 1; Jane Perlez, *NYT*, same day.

17. "Group of Eight's Kosovo Statement," *NYT*, May 7, 1999.

18. Yemma, *BG*, May 7, 1999.

19. Jane Perlez, *NYT*, May 8, 1999.

20. Steven Erlanger, *NYT*, May 29; Anne Kornblut, *BG*, May 30, 31, 1999.

21. Charles Madigan, *Chicago Tribune*, June 2, 1999.

22. State Department text, "Kosovo Peace Accord," text, *NYT*, June 4, 1999. For the text approved by the Serb Parliament, see AP, June 3, 1999 (translated by AP). The two texts differ slightly. The version approved by Serbia refers to marking but not clearing of minefields. It also has more detail than the State Department version on a "fast and precise timetable for withdrawal." Draft resolution, "UN Resolution on Kosovo: Establishing the Principles of a Political Solution," AP, *NYT*, June 9, 1999.

23. Lead story, *FT*; and Guy Dinmore, *FT*; June 4, 1999.

24. "A Missing Footnote: 'NATO at the Core'," *NYT*, June 9, 1999. The rest reiterates Russia's position, cited above from *FT*, June 4.

25. Katherine Seelye, *NYT*, June 12, 1999.

26. "Key Points," lead headline; interviewer, questioning Secretary of State Albright; Stephen Lee Myers with Craig Whitney, *NYT*, June 4. Staff, *WSJ*, June 4. Kevin Cullen, *BG*, June 6; Michael Gordon, *NYT*, June 11, 1999. One effort to show that the compromise was a "worse deal" is that the international security presence is to be much larger than the NATO occupation force of the Rambouillet Agreement, which is true, but of little concern to Serbia, one would assume: occupation is occupation. The larger force, with greater costs for NATO, is one of the "staggering costs" of the bombardment and the Serbian violence that followed it.

27. For more on these matters, see *Towards a New Cold War, Deterring Democracy*, and sources cited.

28. Steven Pearlstein, "Jamie Shea, NATO's Persuasive Force," *WP*, June 10, 1999.

29. Editorials, *NYT*, June 4, 8; Blaine Harden, "Surprising Lesson: Bombing Can Work," *NYT*, June 5; Elizabeth Becker and David Rohde, Harden, *NYT*, June 6, 1999.

30. *NYT*, June 11, 1999.

31. Editorial, "Summing up Kosovo," *BG*, June 8; David Nyhan, "NATO wins the war," *BG*, June 8; Fred Kaplan, *BG*, June 6, 1999.

32. Lewis, "When Praise is Due," *NYT*, June 12, 1999; *NYT*, April 21, 24, 1975; Dec. 27, 1979. On the sudden conversion of hawks to "long-time opponents of the war" after the Tet offensive convinced the business community that it was no longer worth pursuing, and the radical revision of their earlier accounts by Kennedy memoirists, see *Rethinking Camelot*, chap. 3.

33. John Rielly, *American Public Opinion and U.S. Foreign Policy 1999* (Chicago Council on Foreign Relations, 1999), a regular series. As of 1999, the figure was 63%. For many years it hovered around 70%, astonishing figures for an open question, particularly when respondents are drawing the conclusion in virtual isolation, the conception being inexpressible and unthinkable, under Orwell's maxim. One can only guess what the figures would be if the rigid doctrinal framework were penetrable.

34. Keegan, *Daily Telegraph*, June 4, 1999; Richard Hudson, *WSJ*, Feb. 5, 1991.

35. See chap. 3, note 47, and text.

36. *FT*, June 4, 1999.

37. Stuart Chreighton Miller, *"Benevolent Assimilation"* (Yale 1992).

38. Yemma, "Reclaiming of Kosovo will be a complex task," *BG*, June 10, 1999.

39. Human Rights Watch, *Palestinian Self-Rule Areas: Human Rights Under the Palestinian Authority*, Sept. 1997, detailing "widespread arbitrary and abusive conduct" by the transformed PLO, with those interrogated "commonly tortured," leading to many deaths in custody, scores of secret summary judgments, interference with the press, and other abuses. The record has become much worse since, reviewed in particular depth by Palestinian and Israeli human rights organizations.

40. Deborah Sontag, "Indispensable Man," *NYT*, Dec. 14, 1998. On the reality, see Norman Finkelstein, "Security Occupation: the Real Meaning of the Wye River Memorandum," *New Left Review* (Nov./Dec. 1998), revised Feb. 1999; Nasser Aruri, "The Wye Memorandum: Netanyahu's Oslo and Unreciprocal Reciprocity," *J. of Palestine Studies* XXVIII.2 (Winter 1999); documents appear here as well. Also David Sharrock, *Guardian Weekly*, Jan. 17, 1999. Reviewed in the 1999 edition of *Fateful Triangle*.

41. On the Pascalian technique and its contemporary applications, see *Necessary Illusions*, chap. 4.

42. Franz Schurmann, Peter Dale Scott, and Reginald Zelnick, *The Politics of Escalation in Vietnam* (Fawcett World Library, 1966); Scott, *The War Conspiracy* (Bobbs-Merrill, 1972).

43. See my 1973 article reprinted in *Towards a New Cold War*; and for summary in a more general context, *Manufacturing Consent*.

44. Headlines in *New York Times*, Anthony Lewis. For detailed review as events were proceeding, see *Culture of Terrorism* (1988), *Necessary Illusions* (1989), *Deterring Democracy* (1991).

45. See chap. 1, note 33; chap. 2, note 21; and text.

46. Elizabeth Becker, "Kosovo Talks Break Down as Serbs Balk Over Details: NATO Will Step Up Bombing," *NYT*, June 7, 1999; also Craig Whitney, *NYT*, same day. Kevin Cullen, "Serbs seen pressing for role by UN," June 8, 1999.

47. Becker, *NYT*, June 8, 1999.

48. Jane Perlez, "Russians Balking as Gains are Made on Kosovo Talks," *NYT*, June 8; John Broder, *NYT*, same day.

49. Craig Whitney, *NYT*, June 8.

50. R.W. Apple, *NYT*, June 8, 1999. The "missing footnote" is also upgraded from NATO preference to fact in the accompanying article by Jane Perlez. See chapter 3, note 81.

51. Anne Kornblut and David Filipov, Filipov, *BG*, June 12. John Kifner and Steven Lee Meyers, Steven Erlanger, Michael Gordon, *NYT*, June 12, 1999.

52. Blaine Harden, *NYT*, June 8; Kevin Cullen, *BG*, June 11, 1999.

53. Kevin Cullen, "Democracy activism: a war casualty," *BG*, May 26, citing "pro-Western activists" who describe the "democracy movement" as one of the first casualties of the bombing. BHHRG analysts, May 22, 1999. "Media Focus," Feb. 17, 1999, London, a regular review of media in the FRY, highly critical of Milosevic and his repression and atrocities.

54. For detailed review and comparison, see *Necessary Illusions*, Appendix V.6–8. On the remarkably high reliance on independent news sources and dissident publications in the former Soviet Union, contrasting sharply with the situation in the free societies, see James Miller and Peter Donhowe, *Washington Post Weekly*, Feb. 17, 1986. For discussion in a more general context, see *Letters from Lexington*, chap. 17.

55. Guy Dinmore, *FT*, April 10/11; April 24. The April 23 strikes were condemned by the International Federation of Journalists and other media organizations. *Ibid.*, Kevin Cullen, *BG*, April 24, 1999. On the Chinese reaction to the killing of three Chinese journalists by NATO bombing, scarcely reported here apart from concerns over state-organized anti-Americanism, see the reports from *China Daily* in the advertising supplement, *WP Weekly*, May 31, 1999.

56. Daniel Pearl, "Propaganda War: A Bosnian TV Station Staffed by Serbs, Runs Afoul of U.S., NATO," *WSJ*, May 13, 1999, lead story; apparently ironic.

57. William Preston, Edward Herman, and Herbert Schiller, *Hope & Folly: the United States and UNESCO 1945–1985* (Minnesota, 1989).

Chapter Six
Why Force?

1. On Saddam and the Kurds, see Randal, *op. cit.*. On the 1991 events and the official justifications, *Deterring Democracy* and later publications, updating, including *Powers and Prospects*. Albright on Iraq, Serge Schmemann, "The Critics Now Ask: After Missiles, What?," *NYT*, Dec. 18, 1998; Albright on Indonesia, my "L'Indonésie," *Le Monde*

diplomatique, June 1998. On 1958, see Kahin and Kahin, *op. cit.* PKI, the Communist Party of Indonesia, Harold Crouch, *Army and Politics in Indonesia* (Cornell, 1978). Reaction to the 1965 slaughter, *Year 501*, chap. 5.

2. Steven Erlanger, "Belgrade 'Targets' Find Unity 'From Heaven'," *NYT*, March 30; Matic, Op-ed, *NYT*, April 3; Ryan, "NATO bombs raze dreams of democracy," *BG*, April 4, 1999. Vojvodina, chap. 2, notes 25, 26 and text. Matic award, *Media Focus*; see chap. 5, note 53.

3. See Gleijeses, *op. cit.*, for one telling illustration, based on close analysis of a rich record concerning Guatemala.

4. Gellman, William Drozdiak, *WP Weekly*, March 29, 1999, and many other reports.

5. Harden, "The Long Struggle That Led the Serbian Leader to Back Down," *NYT*, June 8, 1999.

6. Elaine Sciolino and Ethan Bronner, "How a President, Distracted by Scandal, Entered Balkan War," *NYT*, April 18, 1999.

7. Keegan, *Daily Telegraph*, May 21; Pfaff, *BG*, April 12, 1999. On his subsequent interpretations, see pp. 93–4.

8. Jane Perlez, "For Albright's Mission, More Problems and Risk," *NYT*, June 7, 1999, reporting the assessments of Secretary of State Albright and assorted experts.

9. See Irwin Wall, "U.S., Algeria, and the Fourth French Republic," *Diplomatic History*, Fall 1994.

10. See *World Orders*, chap. 3.

11. Thomas Ricks and Anne Marie Squeo, *WSJ*, June 4; Ross Kerber, *BG*, June 4; Peter Thal Larsen, "Kosovo conflict highlights real winners in wars," *FT*, June 1, 1999.

12. Cited by Frank Kofsky, *Harry Truman and the War Scare of 1948* (St. Martin's Press, 1993). For more on the topic, see *World Orders* and sources cited, only a fraction of the rich and important story, primarily scattered in technical monographs. For a lucid account of socialization of risk and other leading features of the international economy, see Robin Hahnel, *Panic Rules!* (South End, 1999). On the general background, see Richard DuBoff, *Accumulation and Power* (M. E. Sharpe, 1989).

13. Daniel Pearl, *WSJ*, June 4; Charles Pretzlik, *FT*, June 6, 1999.

14. Craig Whitney, "European Union Vows to Become Military Power," *NYT*, June 4; Warren Hoge, "Europeans Impressed By Their Own Unity," *NYT*, June 4, 1999.

15. Mary Leonard, "'Victory for a safer world'," lead headline, BG, June 11, 1999.

16. Lloyd, FT, Jan. 19–20, 1991. On world opinion after the Gulf war, see my article in Collateral Damage, op. cit.

17. Karim El-Gawhary, "NATO's bill of rights," Al-Ahram Weekly, May 27, 1999.

18. Gilboa, see chap. 1, note 15.

19. Schiff, Ha'aretz, June 11, 1999.

20. The Hindu, May 12, 1999.

21. Editorials, Times of India, May 8; Hindu, April 9, April 22, 1999.

22. Editorial, Hindu, June 7, 1999.

23. Huntington, FA, March/April 1999.

24. Rebecca Johnson, "Troubled Treaties: Is the NPT tottering?"; Michael Crepon, "CTBT [Comprehensive Test Ban Treaty] deadline nears," same heading; Bulletin of the Atomic Scientists, March/April 1999.

25. Appendix 2 of Nuclear Futures: Proliferation of Weapons of Mass Destruction and US Nuclear Strategy, by Hans Kristensen (British American Security Information Council) (BASIC), Basic Research Report 98.2, March 1998. For excerpts, see AP, "Irrationality suggested to intimidate US enemies," BG, March 2, 1998; my "Rogue States," Z, April 1998.

26. BASIC Research Report, Appendix 1.

27. Gilboa, op. cit.. On the Israeli theory, see Fateful Triangle, 464ff.

28. National Security Strategy of the United States, the White House, March 1990. See Deterring Democracy, chap. 1, for excerpts.

29. See Phythian, op. cit., 41.

30. Quotes here and below from planning documents cited in the BASIC study.

31. On the predictions by prominent analysts, and the recognition, see Deterring Democracy, chaps. 3, 4. Another prediction, also cited, was that Third World interests could now be freely ignored.

32. Ibid., chap. 7, for some comparisons.

33. Ibid., chap. 3, for illustration.

34. Karen Lissakers, Banks, Borrowers, and the Establishment (Basic Books, 1993), 201. On how the system works, see Hahnel, op. cit.

35. Michelle Faul, AP, Feb. 10. Dina Ezzat, reporting from Jamaica, Al-Ahram Weekly, Feb. 11–17, 1999.

36. Nexis search by David Peterson for the three-week period from Feb. 1–21, 1999 (the meeting was Feb. 10–12). His search found extensive coverage in the South.

Chapter Seven
World Order and Its Rules

1. Schmemann, "Now, Onward to the Next Kosovo. If There Is One," *NYT* "Week in Review," June 6, 1999.

2. *Proceedings of the American Society of International Law* 13, 14 (1963), cited by Louis Henkin, *How Nations Behave* (Council on Foreign Relations, Columbia, 1979), 333–4; Trachtenberg, *op. cit.*, citing 1961 Acheson Report (Kennedy Library).

3. Weller, *op. cit.*

4. *ASIL Newsletter*, March–April 1999. Vagts, *op. cit.*

5. Ian Bickerton, *FT*, June 3; Marlise Simons, *NYT*, June 3, 1999. The legal basis for the charges was absurd, as was the time frame stipulated, both crafted to avoid countercharges against Yugoslavia.

6. Crook, Assistant Legal Advisor for United Nations Affairs, U.S. Deptartment of State, Counsel and Advocate; Court Proceedings, released May 30, 1999.

7. See *Human Rights Violations in the United States* (New York: HRW/ACLU, Dec. 1993). For review, "The U.S. and the 'Challenge of Relativity'" (see chap. 3, note 71).

8. Shultz, "Moral Principles and Strategic Interests," U.S. Department of State, *Current Policy* No. 820, speech of April 14, 1986, timed to coincide with Washington's terrorist bombing of Libya. See *Necessary Illusions*, App. V.2. Sofaer, "The United States and the World Court," U.S. Department of State, Bureau of Public Affairs, *Current Policy* No. 769 (Dec. 1985). For more extensive quotes, see my "'Consent without Consent': Reflections on the Theory and Practice of Democracy," *Cleveland State Law Review* 44.4 (1996).

9. 1949, Corfu Channel Case. Epigraph to Haas, *op. cit.*

10. Kevin Done, *FT*, March 27/28, 1999.

11. Blair, "A New Generation" (see p. 3).

12. Bull, "Justice in international relations," *1983 Hagey Lectures*, U. of Waterloo, Waterloo, Ont., 1983, 1–35. Henkin, *op. cit.*, 144–5; also cited by Murphy, *op. cit*, as of particular significance.

Index

About the Author

NOAM CHOMSKY is a long-time political activist, writer and Institute Professor of Linguistics at the Massachusetts Institute of Technology. He is the author of numerous books on U.S. foreign policy, international affairs and the media. His most recent books include an updated version of *The Fateful Triangle*, *Profit Over People* and *The Common Good*.